Heavenly Encounters

PERSONAL EXPERIENCES WITH GOD

Gerry Dodson

ISBN: 1523698470
ISBN 13: 9781523698479

Dedication

This book is dedicated to those who were willing to share their stories of God's care over His creation. These are your neighbors, your friends or your church family, ordinary people who experienced His healing power, His protection, His provision for their needs or divine guidance. May you be blessed as you read their stories.

God Bless You,

Gerry Dodson

Acknowledgements

Gerry Dodson

It is with a grateful heart that I acknowledge all those that helped with this project. At the book signing of my first published book, I mentioned how nice a corporate book would be if we could get people to tell their stories. Steve Lester, a brother in Christ came to me and said, "I think the idea of a corporate book is wonderful." With his encouragement and help from him and his wife Tama, we began to collect stories from those who were willing to share. Those two did most of the computer work. Thanks to both of you. Anna Lester Evans and Millie Dodson Felice were so gracious to help with the grammar correction and editing. I appreciate you both. My daughter, Gail, helped me on my computer, finding what I lost and sending emails. Thanks, honey. My daughter-in-law, Susan Dodson is a real treasure. She had all the stories re-typed, did the final editing and dealt with the publishing company. Susan, what would I do without you? You have been a very present help in my time of need. Lastly, a very special thanks to all those who were willing to tell their stories so others would know of God's love and care for all His creation. May you be blessed as you read the following stories and may God be glorified.

God Provides

My God shall supply all your needs, according to His riches in glory. (Philippians 4: 19)

Not only does He provide for our needs but wants to give us the desires of our hearts. He can give exceedingly, abundantly above what we ask or even think.

Healing

He sent His word and healed them and delivered them from their destruction. (Psalms 107:20)

The following stories are from people just like you. Following accidents or serious illness, the Lord restored them to health. Most of the stories in both the Old Testament and the New Testament required an act of faith on the part of the person in need of healing. Naaman, the Syrian, was a leper. He went to Elisha for healing and was told to dip seven times in the Jordan River. He was angry and refused until his servant encouraged him to do so. When he obeyed, he was healed. The story is found in the book of II Kings, chapter five. When the children of Israel complained about Moses and God, poisonous serpents were sent among them. God instructed Moses to put the likeness of the serpent on a pole and to tell the people to look at it if they were bitten. Those who looked were healed; those who didn't look died. (Numbers 21:8). In Luke 17, ten lepers came to Jesus for healing. He told them to go show themselves to the priest as required by the law. As they went they were healed.

In James 5:14-16, there are very clear instructions for us today if we need healing. " Is any sick among you? Let him call for the elders of the church; let them pray over him, anointing him with oil in the name of the Lord: And the prayer of faith shall save the sick, and the Lord shall raise him up; and if he has committed sins, they shall be forgiven him. Confess your faults one to another, and pray for one another, that you may be healed.

Protection

Angels are only servants. They are spirits sent from God to care for those who will receive salvation. (Hebrews 1:14 NLT)

I wonder how many times we have been in extreme danger and our unseen protector was on the job. Only eternity will reveal that to us.

He Guides Us

In the book of Exodus, the Spirit of God gave skilled men explicit instructions for building the tabernacle and it contents. There can be no doubt that

God has been involved in the invention of machinery and technology that we enjoy today. Medical advancements, space travel and beautiful buildings came into being because of the spirit God placed in mankind.

The Holy Spirit given to those who believe in Jesus will bring insight and guidance when we are unsure of what should be done.

The Joplin Tornado

By: Naomi Burke

On Sunday, May 22nd, 2011 in Joplin, Missouri, the day dawned heavy with humidity. Weather forecasters were predicting thunderstorms with the possibility of a tornado. This is quite common in the spring in our part of the country so we spent our day as usual, not knowing that many lives would be changed forever before the day ended.

Don, my husband, and I were nearing retirement after fifty plus years serving as missionaries to the Native American population. We were living in Joplin because that was the headquarters of our denomination. We had already bought a retirement home in Broken Bow, Oklahoma since we had lots of family and friends there. In fact, that is where we had grown up so we would just be going back home.

Late in the evening the tornado sirens started going off. We went into the bathroom, as we had no cellar or safe room. I sat down on the toilet, and Don stood beside me with his arm around me. The tornado hit our home, leaving total devastation all around us but neither of us was injured. The glass shower door had shattered and my hair was full of broken glass.

"Where will we go?" asked Don. We had planned to go to the oldest Pentecostal church, but so much debris kept us "staying with our stuff". Nelda, our daughter, lived in a mobile home three miles south of town. When storms came up, she usually came to our house because she felt it was safer. After contacting her, we were told she was safe and unharmed and that she would come to us as soon as possible. She had to dodge debris and wait for some of the roads to be cleared before she could arrive. When she arrived, she asked where was my purse and Don's billfold? We hadn't given any thought to our belongings at the time. After a brief search, she picked up a corner of the mattress and by some miracle; it lay there untouched with all the contents intact. Don's wallet was found against a partly standing wall with all the contents still in it as well. Tearfully, we began to count our blessings.

In a church on our block, five were found dead. In our area 22 people perished. Someone driving by asked "Is anyone alive in here?" We all answered yes. The voice said they would be back, but they had an injured man who needed medical attention. When they returned, we climbed over all the debris and got in their vehicle. They took us to our church, dodging all the junk on the streets. When we reached the church, standing in the alley was our dear pastor with two couples who we didn't know. The couples asked us to come home with them since we had nowhere to go. I was cold, dripping wet, and had glass in my hair. I raised my hand to heaven and said "Oh, Jesus you still have a church." Matthew 16:18b says, "I will build my church and the gates of Hell will not prevail against it." Frankly, I felt like we had been there.

Inside the church, we were wrapped in warm blankets and given something to eat and drink. We were treated like royalty, two dripping, almost numb King's Kids.

Nelda met volunteers on the road amid all the trash and debris. She took us to her house where she ran warm water through my hair to get the glass out. She didn't attempt to scrub my scalp for fear of cutting me. She finally got all the glass out. After a warm bath and clean pajamas and extra clothes, we realized how blessed we were not to have lost a family member. Nelda never once acted like she was ready for us to move on or as if we were imposing on her. Through the years, many people have said to her that she should have been a nurse.

Folks were so kind and considerate and things started to return to fairly normal for us. We moved to Broken Bow and found the people there to be loving and helpful also. Four years after our tornado experience Don celebrated his 86th birthday and we also celebrated 68 years of marriage. How blessed we have been. Another miracle, or some may call it a coincidence, that came out of the storm was that our son, Mike, had volunteered to move his Aunt Venoy to Tennessee. If he had been home that day, he might have been in that brass bed that was devastated in the tornado.

When asked why I'm still working, my reply is, "For quitting time and pay day." Selfish? Not at all. "Be though faithful unto death (quitting time) and I will give thee a crown of life. (Pay day)."

TO GOD BE THE GLORY.

How God Saved My Life

By: Esta O. Callaham

It was December 1983, the worst winter we had experienced in years. We had ice and snow on the ground and freezing weather. Our church choir had been working on a singing Christmas tree at our church on Broadway. We had purchased the land to build the new church building that is located today at 1501 S. Park Drive and risers had been constructed for our singing tree at the new location. We were all excited to sing on the property.

I had planned a Christmas party at home for the choir after the singing. I had left home in a hurry without my scarf and cap and I was going across the road to call and tell my family to bring it to me. I don't remember being hit by a car at all. I do remember waking up in an ambulance. Our pastor Don Ramsey was with me. He prayed for me, and I passed out again. I was taken to DeQueen, Arkansas, and then they transferred me to Wadley Hospital in Texarkana, Texas. I remember waking up in the emergency room and telling them to sew me up good. I also remember when they drilled the screw in at my knee to put me in traction. My injuries were: cuts on my face, a broken nose, jaw, teeth, and both sides of my ankle and femur bones were broken.

I was put in traction and was told I would have surgery in two or three days. My, what pain I started experiencing! I knew I was dying. I had blood clots in my lungs close to my heart and the surgery was canceled. No pain medicine could take away that pain. My family was called in, and they had a hard time driving as the roads were covered in ice. I can still feel my mom's hand on my head praying and asking God to spare my life. My church family and many others were praying also. My mom's favorite scripture that she leaned upon was: Proverbs 3:5–6, "Trust in the Lord with all thine heart; and lean not unto thine own understanding. In all thy ways acknowledge Him, and He will direct thy paths."

One of the hardest things for me to bear was being in traction flat on my back and totally dependent upon others for all my needs. I'm so thankful for my sister-in-law, Linda Coleman, who was there for all of my personal needs. Little things mean a lot when you're lying flat on your back, your leg in traction, and can only move your hands. I was wearing only a hospital gown. I had a special friend that called me and wanted to do something for me. I expressed how much I missed wearing underwear and felt so naked. Mildred Smalling said, "I'll take care of that", but I didn't know what she meant. She had her friend make me underwear with Velcro on the sides. Oh! How good that felt not to feel so exposed. I know it was vanity, but little things mean a lot when you were help-less. I thank my friend for being sensitive to my personal needs.

A specialist was called in to consult about the blood clot. They talked about stents, but decided it was too close to my heart. The decision was made to give me blood transfusions and keep my blood thin. I don't recall how many pints of blood I was given but it went on for days. The pain never went away. Dr. Knight was my orthopedic doctor, and he never missed a day of seeing me, even on Christmas Day.

When I had been at the hospital for six weeks, they wanted to do a spinal block in order to repair my ankle on the left side. Because I was still in traction, they couldn't reach my back, so they were going to take me back to my room without doing surgery. I prayed, "Oh God! Help me to turn so I can have the surgery." I knew there was a possibility that if I couldn't have the surgery I could be left with the shorter leg and would also walk with a limp. My anesthesiologist said, "Honey we are going to make this work", and she did. They put screws in my ankle and added a cast. Thank God for Christian doctors.

After that, I was back in my room with a cast up to my knee and still in trac-tion. They would come to my room every Monday to x-ray my femur bone and see if it was healing. I always received a bad report. My sister-in-law who lived in Dallas, Texas, stayed with me all the time I was in the hospital. She had a group of ladies from her church come see me and pray for me. They had prayer bells from heaven! I felt the bone in my leg move, but I only told her at that time. The x-ray technicians came in Monday to see if I was making progress. This time they said my femur bone was improving and healing. My sister-in-law looked at me, and we knew what had happened. Praise the Lord, my leg was healing. God is so good. I had told many people of this miracle. I know God answered our prayers.

In conclusion, I had five casts and went home nine weeks later with a cast up to my waist. God had healed the blood clots. The stitches in my face, jaw, and nose had healed. My teeth would be replaced later. I had to learn to walk again and was in therapy for one whole year. My sweet daughter had to plan her wedding in June by herself. I was walking with support at her wedding. I had lost about 25 pounds in the hospital, but with the help of the Lord and lots of pain and tears I persevered. I was determined to walk without a limp and with the Lord's help, He saw me through this trying time. He said to ask and you shall receive. I stood upon that promise and I received that blessing.

I see my therapist from time to time mostly at the mall or at a restaurant. She calls me her miracle lady. I know I'm a miracle and God has given me a gift to recognize when people are suffering. I'm very sensitive to that spirit and use it for the glory of God. Our God is a God of miracles, and I am a living example of it. Thank you for letting me share my testimony. I pray it will be a blessing to those who need to be encouraged.

Faithful God

By: Florence Bell Campbell

D o Christians have times almost too hard to bear? Do bad things happen to good people? Yes, every Christian will go through times too difficult to bear alone but as children of God He walks us through them, holding our hands and giving us strength.

I'm Florence Bell Campbell and I'm going to share one of my most difficult times when God walked me through a nine month trial and gave me heavenly strength that still amazes me almost 24 years later, proving He is good all the time; even the darkest hours of our worst times.

The Lord is our Rock, our firm Foundation, our Cornerstone and He is forever unchanging. The following scripture from the amplified Bible is one I hung onto during this time. Psalm 18:1-2 says, "I love you fervently and devoted, oh, Lord, my strength. The Lord is my rock, my fortress, and my deliverer; my God, my keen and firm strength in whom I will trust and take refuge, my shield, and the horn of my salvation, my high tower."

There have been many times God has truly brought me back from death's door. This time was not only myself, but also my precious husband, DeMoine Bell. This trial lasted nine months and ended with the tragedy of his death. God not only chose to bring me through, but He also gave me strength to do things I never could have done on my own.

March 1991 was the beginning of this long, hard journey, but also the beginning of God going ahead of me and working His miracles and grace. He walked through it with me.

Life seemed perfect for us. We were in Falcon Heights, TX, where his job had taken us. We had my mother with us. She was in failing health and could not be left alone. We were keeping her so she could avoid going to a nursing home.

As far as we knew DeMoine's health was perfect. Our friends, Ward and Gerry Dodson, had come to visit so they could fish together on Falcon Lake. Ward's health was failing and he wanted to fish one more time with his buddy. They fished hard for several days and enjoyed every minute of it. It would be their last fishing trip together.

On Friday, we had a call from my Sister, Naomi Tipps. She and her husband, Terry, were home from Spain where they served as missionaries. They wanted to see Mother, but their schedule did not allow them the time to come to South Texas. They wanted us to bring Mother and meet them halfway. We loaded up the next morning, met them, and spent the night visiting with them. The next morning they took Mom back to Oklahoma and we headed back to Falcon Heights. Little did I know this was God's first miracle for me in getting Mom back to Oklahoma where she would be safe. God knew what would happen the next day.

The day after we returned home, our day began like any other, with the exception that Mom wasn't here with us. DeMoine said we should go fish a while since it was such a beautiful day. That sounded good to me, so we went and fished for a few hours. We came back to the trailer about lunchtime. DeMoine decided to leave the boat hooked up to the pickup truck so we could go fish again that evening when it was cooler.

He put some steaks and potatoes on the grill and decided to mow the lawn while they cooked, not knowing what would happen in less than an hour. This was the beginning of a few miracles of strength God gave me that day and many days to follow. DeMoine had been mowing awhile and suddenly the lawn mower didn't sound right. I ran to the window to see what was wrong. DeMoine was on his knees, his hands still holding the running lawn mower, the blades spinning in the air.

When I got outside to him, it was apparent he was having a heart attack. I was a lab and x-ray technician and I knew all too well what was happening. What I didn't know was how I could do what must be done. I knew how important time was in getting him to the hospital. At that moment, I realized the miracle of Mother being safe in Oklahoma.

After I got DeMoine's hand loose from the mower and shut it off, I got him comfortable on the ground. I called the hospital, asked them to get our doctor, and said I would get DeMoine there as soon as I could. They wanted to send the EMS, but I told them they would never find us. We were in a gated trailer park, forty miles from Rio Grande General Hospital. I hung up, praying as I returned to my husband, trying to get him up off of the ground and to the pickup. That's when I realized the boat was still hooked up to the pickup, and it was quite a distance from us. I tried to get the boat unhooked, but it was on uneven ground and in a bind. I couldn't budge it.

Usually there were other people in the park. That day no one was to be seen. I began to cry out to God, telling Him, "Your Word says, as my day is, so shall my strength be." Then I tried again and got the boat unhooked. I thanked God, lowered the boat, and drove the pickup to where DeMoine lay on the ground, white as a ghost and lifeless. I tried to lift him, but I couldn't. He was six feet tall and 220 pounds of dead weight. My 85 pounds didn't have enough strength to get him up. My heart sank, knowing I needed to be on the way to the hospital.

Desperately, again I cried out to God the same prayer and added, "You said you would never leave me or forsake me in my time of trouble," and He didn't. It is still mind-boggling to me how I got DeMoine off the ground and into that big truck. God's angels had to have helped me. I know that for sure. Truly, God's grace and strength are sufficient to meet our needs.

As I drove those forty miles to the hospital, I had never driven that fast or prayed so hard that I could get him to the hospital safe and alive. Again, God answered my prayers. As I pulled into the ER entrance, the doctor was waiting for us. He ran to the truck and said, "Who helped you load him?" "The good Lord did," I said. "Maybe there are miracles after all," he replied.

After they got DeMoine into the hospital, blood work and tests revealed it was indeed a massive heart attack, along with other complications like a genetic heart condition. The staff said as soon as they could get his vitals stable, they would transport him to a bigger hospital in McAllen, Texas. They would have a surgical team ready to do bypass surgery. They let me ride in the ambulance with them to McAllen. A medic worked on DeMoine all the way.

When we arrived, they took him directly to surgery. The results of the arteriogram showed that he had two one hundred percent blockages and one ninety percent blockage. In the process of the test, an artery was punctured. They told me the artery was curved.

I felt like something was wrong because as I waited, a nurse was in and out with blood on her scrubs. I asked her if something was wrong. She said, "The doctor will tell you later." I waited and prayed. I didn't know a single person. I was almost one thousand miles from two of our daughters and two thousand miles from the other one. Neither the girls nor anyone else knew where I was or what had transpired in the last few hours. This happened before everyone had cell phones and I was waiting for the doctor to tell me something before I called them.

In the meantime, I walked up and down the halls, praying. It was just God and I as I prayed and quoted scripture. I had never lived in such total dependence on God. I felt His presence. It was as if His arms were around me, holding me close and comforting me. I'll never forget that. What do people do without Him?

They took DeMoine to ICU and gave him three pints of blood. The doctor came and told me he needed triple bypass surgery. He felt DeMoine was too weak for surgery right then and would wait until morning. He also said he was critical. After the doctor finished explaining everything to me, I had the dreaded job of calling the girls and DeMoine's parents. Having to give them that news was hard. The next three weeks continued to be hard.

The girls all said they would fly in as soon as they could get flights. That lifted my spirits, knowing they were coming. I spent the long night in the ICU waiting room, praying and waiting. DeMoine was taken to surgery early the next morning. It was a long surgery, but thank God, he came through it and so did I. The girls got there that day and that was such a blessing to me. Their presence, love, and support were priceless.

DeMoine's next few days in ICU were a roller coaster. He did not do well. Easter fell on April 19th that year, which was also DeMoine's birthday. He had taken pneumonia. His condition wasn't good, so we didn't get to have our short visits in ICU. We spent most of the day in the hospital chapel. Again, God heard and answered our prayers.

Over the next few days, he began to improve. I got to take him home a week later with an arterial defibrillator. They couldn't keep his heart in rhythm. He had to take two kinds of heart medicine every three hours, around the clock. We set the alarm and were faithful to his schedule, but at the most unexpected times I would have to rush him to the hospital so that they could get his heart back in rhythm. Life was like a ticking time bomb! In those days, I truly learned the meaning of, "I can do all things through Christ who strengthens me." Christ was my strength and sustainer.

In July, DeMoine wanted to go see all the children and grandchildren. I could feel this was very important to him. We traveled to Woodward, Oklahoma to spend time with Cheryl and her family, and then on to Blackwell, Oklahoma to our parents and siblings. From there, we went to Princeton, Minnesota to visit Sonja and family, then on to Los Alamos, New Mexico to Brenda's family. We spent a week at each place. It was such a special time and leaving was always difficult. I could tell by how DeMoine acted and the things he said that he felt like it was his last time to be with them. The miracle of those four weeks was that I did not have to rush him to the hospital. I thanked God every day for that blessing. God gave him his heart's desire of spending time with the family. God is good.

We returned to Falcon in late August. The weather was almost always nice there. We would take walks and DeMoine took his meds. We counted every day as another blessing. In late September, he was depressed. That wasn't like him. I called his parents to see if they wanted to come for a visit. They agreed and he enjoyed their visit. We had several good days with the folks.

Columbus Day fell on October 14th that year. We all decided to drive into Rio Grande City to shop and buy groceries. That was the nearest place for good shopping. We ended up taking longer than usual and as we were driving home, I kept looking at my watch, not wanting to be late for his medicines. He could always read my mind. He patted me on the leg and said, "Relax, worrywart, we are almost home." Only seconds later, my whole world changed.

11

I didn't understand why DeMoine was suddenly driving so fast. I looked at him to ask why and when I did I realized what was happening. His arms and legs were stretched out, stiff on the steering wheel and gas pedal. He was looking straight ahead like he was in a trance. I couldn't pull his leg off the gas pedal. That is when I realized he was having another heart attack. I remember saying, "Jesus, Jesus," and us leaving the highway, crashing through a fence, and literally flying across a pasture. We came to a deep ravine and our car turned end over end three and a half times. It stopped when a huge tree near the bottom of the ravine hit the windshield. I remember a loud crash and nothing else for hours. At that point, all of us were probably unconscious.

God was watching over us by allowing a man about a mile away to hear the loud crash. He had gas wells and thought there had been an explosion. He notified the authorities and they began to search for what had happened. I understand it took them about three hours to find us. A rancher that owned the land was helping with the search. He found the fence broken down and followed the path of smashed sage grass. It was about a mile from the highway to the ravine. When he found the wrecked car, he called for EMS and the Jaws of Life. He thought we were all dead.

The next thing I remember was hearing loud noises and someone was trying to get me out of my seat belt. Someone said, "She is so small, let's take her out through the window." They did that and I remember being laid on the ground, face down, as I was bleeding from the nose, mouth and ears. The pain was horrible throughout my body. They said I was hanging upside down in my seat belt. As the car flipped, I had been banged up pretty badly.

They told me DeMoine's legs were still stiff on the pedal. From the waist down, he was still in the driver's seat. His torso was twisted, lying in the passenger seat. The crash had severed his spine. His parents were smashed between the front and back seats. It took a long time to get them and DeMoine extricated. Everyone was in critical condition, but still alive. There were four ambulances and medics waiting to rush us to the hospital.

DeMoine was paralyzed from the neck down. Doctors performed an eleven-hour surgery, trying to fix him so he could sit up. It didn't work. They put him on a huge rotating table, continually turning him four different ways. All the time he was begging them to unplug the machine and let him die. He would say, "I'm dead already." The doctors said he was a person who couldn't adjust to being paralyzed. He had no head injuries except for a few cuts and bruises. His mind was fine and that made it worse for him.

He prayed to die. On the 17th, his temperature went to 104 degrees and his blood sugar went to 800 plus. He had never had blood sugar problems. He went into a semi-coma condition and his blood pressure was very high. The doctor told me he had coded three times and they shocked him back. He kept calling my name. They wheeled me in to see him so that he could see that I was alive. They also wanted me to tell him it was all right for him to give up if he couldn't live with his condition. I could not bring myself to say it until I prayed. God spoke to my heart that if DeMoine couldn't function being paralyzed, He would give me strength to let him go and live without him. Those were the most difficult words I have ever had to say.

As soon as I told him it was all right for him to go and that God had promised to help me, he coded again. This time, they couldn't bring him back. The doctor said that was all he had been waiting for. On the seventeenth of October, DeMoine entered his rest. He was whole again. Our loss was certainly Heaven's gain.

Mom, Dad, and I had many surgeries. With God's help and strength, we began our journey back to health and began learning to deal with life without our loved one. When the doctor released the folks, they flew back to Blackwell, Oklahoma to continue their difficult journey. They had lost a five-year-old son to leukemia, and now their adored first-born. No parent should have to endure giving up two children.

I had to have more surgeries, but I insisted that my daughters not plan to be with me, as their families needed them more than I. I assured them God would be with me and I would be fine. The next chapter of my life was not easy, but God did give me strength. All of the doctors and nurses were so good to me, as were the employees who worked under DeMoine. The girls and their families called daily. God was right with me 24/7, just as He promised. It was a long and difficult two months that followed, but my relationship with my Heavenly Father was priceless.

The most difficult surgery for me was the reconstruction on my face, my jawbone, and my vocal cords. They were injured by the seat belt. I couldn't talk very well and I could not sing. That broke my heart. Music had always been a big part of my life. I asked the Lord to please let me talk and sing again. It was unreal how calm and peaceful I was before and after the surgery. Medical personnel told me I woke up in recovery asking, "Can I sing now?" When I was fully awake they explained to me that I shouldn't talk any more than necessary and not to sing for at least eight weeks. I was in a full facial cast with two holes to see, two for breathing and one big enough for my faithful straw. That straw and a blender were my closest friends as my jaws were wired together. Everyone said I looked like Casper, the friendly ghost—I guess I did. One day leaving the hospital, a little boy, half scared to death, said, "Mama, there is a real ghost!"

After eight weeks, the cast was removed. I could see, eat real food, talk and yes, I could sing. How I thanked God for His faithfulness! After I was released from the hospital, my church family took turns making sure I had what I needed. Again God was faithful in supplying for my needs. In December, my doctor felt I needed to be near my family and transferred me to doctors in Texarkana, Texas. That made me happy and anxious to be with my family again. I prayed that God would make a way for that to happen, as I wasn't able to drive yet. The answer came a couple of days later when Jim Green, a young man who worked for I.B.W.C., called me. He said he didn't have money for gas or food, but if I would take care of the expenses, he and his wife would take me to Cheryl's house in good old Broken Bow, Oklahoma. I could hardly wait.

We left Falcon on December 12th, planning to be in Broken Bow by the 14th. I wanted to surprise my grandson, Jason, on his birthday. We only got half way when the transmission went out on their car so we didn't get to Broken Bow until December 15th. We had to celebrate a day late, but I was so thankful to be with Cheryl and her family as I healed and started the next chapter of my life on my own. There were many difficult times physically and emotionally, but God walked me through it all.

Satan never stops his attacks. I had two break-ins after I rented a house and was living alone. God protected me and possessions can be replaced. Shortly after that, God led me to a house to buy in a safer area. By that time, I was able to drive to church, which was a real blessing. In December of 1991, my pastor's wife, Sister Jean Woods, asked me to have a ladies' Bible study at my house. I said, "Sure, I have lots of room." I thought Sister Jean would be teaching---she didn't share the news with me that I would be teaching until December 31.

Our first meeting was planned for January 2, 1992 at 9 a.m. Talk about a surprise! I thought my heart might stop. I told God that He would have to help me and give me strength and He did. The first day, we had eight ladies and had a wonderful study. By the time it was over, I was so weak I had to go to bed to rest. As the weeks passed, I continued to gain strength and finally got strong enough to sing. In two months, we had to move to the church fellowship hall because of parking. I had room inside, but parking wasn't safe.

God used the Bible study to help me through the most difficult time of my life. He also gave me such a love and burden for it and the ladies who attended. It simply became my life. January 2, 2015 marked twenty-three years that I had been teaching and the love and burden continues to burn in my heart. We never know what God will do in our lives if we allow Him. Twelve to fifteen ladies from the Bible study have, one by one, finished their race and are in heaven now. They are Heaven's gain and my loss. You might say my relationships with God, my children, my grandchildren, the Bible study ladies and my church family were my life.

A few years after the Bible study began God richly blessed me. He brought another very precious man and his family into my life. Some women never have one good husband and God has blessed me with two. I am truly thankful. We have faced some difficult times with serious health issue, but again, God has been faithful. I can truly say, "God is my refuge and strength, a very present help in time of trouble."(Psalm 46:1) I don't know the next chapter of my life, but I know who holds it in His hands. He has been so faithful to me and He has truly been my strength. I am so grateful for His blessings.

The Man in the Gray Shirt

By: Bob Cheek

I was a field mechanic, employed by the Weyerhauser Company, located in McCurtain County in Southeast Oklahoma. I was sent up north of Mt. Herman to repair a John Deere tree cutter. This was a huge machine with eight feet high tires. I was working on the machine by myself. However, there was another employee on another machine cutting trees. He would cut a row, turn around and come back toward me.

All the hydraulic fluid had leaked out of the machine I was working on. I had to change the hose, and pour in some fluid to check the hose. If there were no leak, I would replace all the fluid. I had to stand on one of the tires to check the fluid. When the fluid hit the bottom of the shift valve, the machine shifted into gear. I suddenly found myself walking on the tire like you would on a rolling barrel. I was going as fast as I could but I couldn't keep up. I knew I was going to end up under that tire and I said, "Well God, I guess this is it."

The next thing I remember is sitting on the ground and watching the machine going off into the woods until it hit a tree. The fellow operating the other machine came over to find out what had happened. When I explained it to him he asked, "Well, where is Hershel?"(He is the man who operated the machine I was working on.) "He hasn't been here all day," I replied. "Who was the guy sitting on the tire? There was a man in a gray shirt sitting on that tire. I saw him every time I came by, " he asked. There can only be one explanation. An angelic being had been sent ahead of time to protect me from an untimely and tragic death. When I remember that incident my heart is filled with thanksgiving to my Lord.

God's Provision

By: Donita Clay

*I*n 1957, my father, Don Burke, was welding next to his Navajo Indian helper in a foot of snow on top of Ganado Mtn. near Gallup, NM when God spoke to his heart. The words were strong and clear and would change the direction of my family's life for sure.

"There's nobody to tell them about Jesus," spoke the Lord.

Dad called Mom, who was living in Broken Bow, OK or "Heaven" as my siblings and I called it. He told her to get packed up; he was coming home in our green 1953 Chevrolet pickup truck to move us to New Mexico to live. I am sure from the stories people tell us that our departure from "Heaven" was not a joyous one. My dad was on the adventure of a lifetime. He had such peace in his heart and the assurance that God had a plan. With the family in tow, Mom drove our 1957 Oldsmobile and Dad pulled the trailer house, which was to be our home for the next several years.

Dad had been promoted to San Juan Division Welding Inspector and would be based at Ciniza Oil refinery just outside of Gallup, near the continental divide. This is where the rainfall runs either to the Atlantic or the Pacific Ocean. Many call it "the top of the world".

The "top of the world" is where God provided a place to park our trailer by an old deserted trading post called the "Wishing Well". Just a little further up the hill, God prepared a place for out first church to be built. When I say prepared I mean it in every sense of the word. The spot was so anointed that a hitchhiker once stopped there as we were building and began weeping uncontrollably. When Mom asked if he would like some people to pray with him, he gave his heart to the Lord there before the church was completed. A local merchant, who wanted his old trading post torn down so it could be replaced with a new one, donated the building materials for the church. He told Dad all the materials would be ours if we would tear it down for him. We three children became expert nail pullers. The larger jobs were for the adults. Many events assured my parents that God was going before them.

God not only prepared the way but His provision for the building materials was confirmation that they were in His will. The Holy Spirit's work of drawing souls to the church was a time of much work, of prayer, and teaching and preaching God's word. It was also a time of trusting God to provide for our family's needs. The harsh desert yielded little other than pinion nuts and tumble weeds. Although the red rocks are so beautiful in the setting sun, the family still must be fed and clothed. Thank the Lord and ladies groups for the missionary boxes that yielded last seasons hand me downs. It was like shopping at Macy's when they came in.

Our food supply is such a wondrous memory to me. Dad hitched a plow to that old pick-up and Mama drove it to dig rows for our garden in the desert. It yielded the tomatoes, corn and other vegetables that a good ole' boy from Hochatown, OK sure knew how to appreciate. At 7,300 feet, the altitude is not suitable for any of those wonderful crops to grow, but God gave his people provision. He took care of our needs, as we trusted Him day by day. I look back and smile at the memory of our garden in the desert. But the real garden in the desert are the souls of six generations of Native Americans who heard about Jesus, gave their hearts to Him, brought their families up to love and serve Him. They then, went out to plant more seed for an even greater harvest of souls. Little is much when God is in it.

My parents were ordained on June 5th, 1958 side by side in the second work they built. That work was completed debt free in Milan, NM and is still operating for the Heavenly Kingdom. In the 58 years of ministry, God has never failed to provide or to keep that which is committed to Him. He will do the same for all who will trust and obey.

Obedient to His Word

By: Lunetta Crow

*I*t happened at a time when I was searching and asking the Lord to help me know how to recognize when it was really HIM speaking or if it was my own emotions and inclinations.

It happened on a Saturday morning just as I was getting up. Just as clearly as if someone had spoken aloud to me, I heard this verse; "Give to him that asks thee and from him that would borrow of thee turn not away." Matthew 5:42. I replied, "Well, nobody has ever asked me for anything, but I will certainly will do it. I truly want to obey you in every way."

Before noon on that very same day, I had a phone call from a lady who is a Christian and was attending our church. She asked me if she could come over and talk to me. I said yes and invited her over. I offered her some coffee, which she declined. I still didn't think anything except that she wanted to talk about her children or some other problem.

We talked for over an hour, after which I asked her to join me for lunch. She declined, stating that she needed to get to the drive-in bank before they closed. After that she got to the real reason she had come to see me.

She needed to borrow enough money to pay for getting care at the ER in Paris, TX. She had gotten quite sick and her children took her to the emergency room. They would not treat her unless she paid prior to treatment a cash payment of $600. Her son's fiancé was the only one who had that kind of money, but it would empty her checking account. She had a certain amount of time to replace the money before consequences would start.

She told me she had started working at Tyson's but had to work a few days before her insurance would pay anything on the claim. I was glad to help her. She went to the restroom while I wrote her out a check.

While writing the check, I felt the Lord telling me to give her cash instead. It was getting late, and I realized that the check might take longer to be verified and deposited.

"I believe it would be better to give you cash instead of a check so your son's fiancé can deposit it in her account more quickly," I said.

She then replied, "You shouldn't keep that much cash here at home!"

I laughed and said that my husband instilled in me that I should always keep "cash on hand" in case of emergencies. She asked if I needed her to sign a note for the money. I said no and turned back into the house. She then left and went on her blessed way.

She couldn't thank me enough. I told her I was happy to help her. That day I was the recipient of a beautiful lesson from the Lord. And today, if I measure my emotions or feelings by His word I cannot make a bad decision.

Lunetta's story took place in late 2013.

God Answers Prayers

By: Jessica (Dodson) Dean

Autumn 1987

In the winter of 1987, a few short months after my 9th birthday and 6 weeks after the birth of my little sister, Millicent, our family relocated from Hugo, Oklahoma to Duluth, Minnesota to start a new chapter of our lives.

It was colder than I had ever imagined possible when we arrived! The white winter wonderland and the "big" city of Duluth were as outlandish to me as a culture shock might be to anyone traveling to a foreign country. We deeply missed the only life we had ever known and all the familiarity of our dear family and friends, but we pulled together as a family, battened down the hatches and braved the rest of our first Minnesota winter together. Winter melted into spring and soon, spring dried out into summer.

Another thing that dried out was my father's wallet. He exhausted his savings and all of his resources working at any job that he could find. He had come to Duluth to start a new church, which he had done, but membership was still very small for the budding church and his salary wasn't even sufficient to pay our monthly household bills.

During that first Minnesota summer, many of my days were spent playing outside with my younger siblings and the neighborhood children. I attempted to make new friends and help my siblings become more accustomed to our new home and feel happy in our new surroundings. I was growing like a weed and as I played, my toes slowly grew out of the end of my shoes. I felt painfully embarrassed as a young girl; I looked around at other girls my age and realized none of them had big awkward toes sticking out of their shoes!

One day, Dad and I were walking through the local K-Mart when I saw something that excited me tremendously. K-Mart was having a shoe sale and the shoes were only $5 a pair! These were the exact shoes that I had been wanting. They looked like the shoes all the other girls wore, only the other girls were silly and frivolous and paid $40 a pair for the name brand. These shoes, minus the name brand, were much cheaper. I wanted them in the worst way.

As soon as I saw them, I exclaimed, "Look, Daddy! It's the shoes I have been wanting!" I looked at him with hopefulness in my big brown eyes and asked him, "Will you please get me these shoes, Daddy?"

I will never forget the look of regret, embarrassment, shame, and disappointment that flashed through my father's eyes when he looked at me. He replied, with tears in his eyes, "I'm so sorry, honey. I would love to get you those shoes if I had any money, but I just don't have any money right now." He even opened his wallet to prove his statement.

On the way home, he told me how bad he felt about not being able to get me the shoes, because he knew how desperately I needed them. He suggested that I pray and ask God to give me the shoes. When we got home, I went to my room, not only to pray for the shoes, but also to ask God to help my dad find a better job that would help provide the things we needed as a family. I, then, wrote a note to my dad so he would have something to put in his wallet.

It said something like: "Dear Daddy, God loves you and so do I. I have been praying that God will give you a better job. Smile. Your struggle is almost over." Unbeknownst to me, my father would carry the letter in his wallet for over a decade. The next day, a card came in the mail from a nice lady who had recently started attending our church. It was just a card to say hello, and at the end, she wrote, "This is so strange and I am also a bit embarrassed to be giving such a small amount, but as I write this note, I feel that the Lord is telling me to send you $5 for shoes." Enclosed in the note was a five-dollar bill.

Almost thirty years later, I can't tell this story without tears streaming down my face. That small gift of $5 meant the world to me and is one of the foundation stones of my faith in God and prayer. God answered my prayer before I ever prayed about it.

You see, my God is faster than the U.S. Postal Service and He wants to supply our every need. Philippians 4:19 says, "And my God will meet all your needs according to the riches of His glory in Christ Jesus. All we need to do is ask Him and have faith." Matthew 17:20 says, "Truly, I tell you, if you have faith as small as a mustard seed, you can say to this mountain, "move from here to there," and it will move. Nothing will be impossible for you."

God spoke to the lady from our church, and because she listened and obeyed, He used her to impact my faith in Him for the rest of my life! Because of the timing and delivery of the answer to my prayer, I knew in my heart that it could only be God who had heard my request and answered it before I had even asked my earthly father.

December 1988

After living in Minnesota for almost two years, things were slowly getting better for our family. The church had grown, and our father had a little more income. My parents were able to purchase a beautiful home that was large enough for all of us, and Christmas was just around the corner.

My mother was thoughtfully and carefully planning her usual beautiful and delicious Christmas dinner. As my parents were discussing side dishes and desserts, I overheard my mother say, "We have a turkey, so we will just have that on Christmas Day."

I liked turkey, but ham had always been my favorite. I asked if we could please get a ham also. Both parents said that ham was much more expensive than turkey, so probably not. They said we couldn't afford it. My father, having a good sense of humor, added, "Maybe you should ask God for one. He certainly heard your prayer and gave you the shoes when you asked Him."

I ran up to my room and got on my knees beside my bed and said, "God, I know we already have food, and I don't want to be selfish, but I really love ham and I am asking you to give us ham for our Christmas dinner. Amen." I believed so much that He was going to bless us with a ham that I could literally taste it.

A few days later, my father opened the front door to get the morning newspaper and he almost tripped over something. It was a grocery bag that contained a big, juicy ham! The better part of that day was filled with exclamations of wonder and joy. All of us were so excited that we had been given a ham for our dinner. God had once again heard my prayer.

That afternoon, a man from our church stopped by to visit and he greatly added to our Christmas cheer by bringing with him a beautiful fruit and nut basket. The basket was quite large, about the size of a wicker laundry basket, and piled high with apples, oranges, pears, nuts in their shells, and many varieties of candy. All of the kids, including me, were so excited we could barely contain ourselves. But we didn't dare touch the edible masterpiece. He stayed and visited with my parents for a while and then wished us all a Merry Christmas and left.

He almost made it to his car before turning around and running back into our house. He said, "Oh my goodness, my wife would have been so upset if I forgot to tell you that there is a ham under the fruit. It will need to be put in the refrigerator!" Then he turned and left again. We were all speechless. God had not only given us one, but two hams!

2 Corinthians 1:15 says, "Since I was so sure of your understanding and trust, I wanted to give you a double blessing by visiting you twice..."

Early 1990s

For as long as I could remember, our family's primary mode of transportation had been the Woody Wagon. Our family consisted of my mother, dad, myself, my sisters (Rachel, Millicent, and Abigail), and my brothers (Jered and Gabriel). For almost my entire childhood, eight people in the family needed a large station wagon or van if we all wanted to ride together.

By this time, my father had mastered the usage of a multi-story cement-parking garage. They were a wonder to see for anyone from a small town. He loved to drive around the loops in the big wagon all the way to the top, partially to make all of us dizzy and also because he loved the view on top.

It was easier to park such a large car on top rather than try to fit inside. On one such trip, our dear old Woody Wagon took her last voyage. After being parked on the top, she never came to life again. My dad tried everything he possibly could think of to get that car running again, but to no avail. He finally called a tow truck and had her towed out. I can still remember him telling the story of how tight the corners were with the length of a tow truck pulling a station wagon around hairpin turns, flight after flight after flight.

Although relieved when that task was accomplished, my dad was also very concerned with how he was going to afford a new car large enough for our family with no notice or warning. Once again, our family was brought to its knees. We prayed and asked God to help us find transportation and a way to pay for it. A short while later, a kind lady in our church came forward and spoke with my parents. She said she knew our car had broken down recently and she felt that God was laying it on her heart to buy our family a car. My parents were overwhelmed by her generosity and kindness. Although they were hesitant to accept such a grand gift, they really had no choice.

They looked at many used car lots and found a few larger wagons and vans, but most of them had many miles on them, and my dad just hated to ask this woman to spend that much. To their surprise, she finally stopped them and said, "Ok, we have looked at what you would get if you were purchasing the car, but now, let's go look at what God wants you to have." She asked them to follow her to the new car lot.

My parents were in complete shock. They left that car lot with a brand-new Chevy station wagon. It was the first new car either of my parents had ever owned. The car came with a rear-facing third row seat, which excited us kids. In one day, our family went from owning a non-reliable, beat-up car, to owning a beautiful brand new car. Ephesians 3:20 says, "Now all glory to God, who is able, through His mighty power at work within us, to accomplish infinitely more than we might ask or think."

The fact that God had answered my prayers for shoes, ham, and now a brand new car had caused my faith in Him to grow. I never doubted His existence or His love because He had proven Himself to be real to me and had showed His love for me at a very early age. I knew that if I asked Him, He would supply my needs and wants.

I am forever grateful for a God that loves us so much that He pours out His blessings on our lives in ways we could never begin to imagine. I try to stay in tune to hear God's voice when He is prompting me to give to someone in need, because others who heard and obeyed God prompting them to give blessed my family so many times throughout my life. I will never be able to repay the many kindnesses that were bestowed on us, so everyday, I look for a new way to pay it forward and help share the love of God with those around me.

God answers our prayers because He loves us and wants us to be happy. He answers large prayers and small prayers to increase our faith in Him and to prove Himself to us and to those around us. Our faith can be new and innocent, such as the faith of a child. (Mark 10:13-16), "Our faith can be small, the size of a mustard seed, but as long as we have enough faith to talk to Him, He will do the rest." (Luke 17:6) "If you have faith as small as a mustard seed, you can say to this mulberry tree, be uprooted and planted in the sea, and it will obey you."

Ministering Spirits

By: Gerry Dodson

*M*y husband, Ward, was an avid fan of Southern Gospel music. We would attend any concert within a reasonable driving distance. Each year in August, in Seminole, Oklahoma there is a three-day event where many of the well-known quartets, trios and musicians perform. We always attended at least one night, usually on Friday. We would meet our friends, Terry and Sue Davidson in Ada and drive on to Seminole together.

Since we were over a hundred miles from home and the singing lasted late into the night we would get a motel room in Ada and drive home on Saturday. It was impossible to get a room in Seminole unless you reserved it months ahead. The event is held outside, weather permitting, and thousands of people attend. It was so inspirational to hear all the beautiful music and to see multitudes of people worshipping the Lord under the starry heavens that God provided.

One year we decided to take our travel trailer and spend the weekend. We arrived on Thursday, got a good parking place where we could see the stage and hear the music. In the daytime we would visit with other campers or shop the junk stores or antique shops. The singing would start about six o'clock in the evening. Each night different groups would perform and we enjoyed them all.

On Sunday morning we got up early, packed all the camping gear and started home. In Ada, we stopped to attend church. After the service we drove to Atoka and stopped for lunch. After eating we walked around awhile for exercise. When we left Atoka, Ward said, "I'm going to set the cruise at 55 mph. That is fast enough pulling this trailer."

We came to an area where the road made a rather sharp curve and went downhill onto a bridge that spanned a ten or twelve foot ravine. Going around

27

the curve our trailer jackknifed. Suddenly, we were going from one side of the highway to the other. The trailer was tipping over so far it was jerking the vehicle around. Everything seemed like it was in slow motion. I didn't have time to pray, but I remember saying, "Oh Jesus". One of two things was going to happen; we would either hit the bridge or end up in a tangled mass at the bottom of the ravine.

We hit the bridge and the trailer tipped over. It hit the bridge rail on one side and tore the back end out of it. The sudden stop caused the vehicle to be jerked around and the front bumper hit the rail on the other side of the bridge. We were crossways on the bridge completely blocking the highway. The stop was so gentle that neither of us was hurt at all. It was like driving into the garage and stopping.

However, we were not out of danger. The highway was a two-lane road and carries a lot of truck traffic. Someone who had been following us had enough forethought to run to the top of the hill and stop traffic. If one of those trucks had come around the curve there would have been no way for him to stop by the time the driver saw us. We had the highway blocked for two hours. The highway patrolmen had to direct traffic to another highway because vehicles were lined up for miles.

That night at church I told our pastor what had happened. He said, "I think the Lord told your guardian angel to get down there quick, there are two old people who really need your help." I have no doubt about that. Hebrews 1:14 says of the angels, "Are they not all ministering spirits, sent forth to minister for them who shall be heirs of salvation?

A Heart of Compassion

By: Hannah Dodson

When I was younger, I felt I had no real testimony. I had been raised in a Christian home with two loving parents and two siblings. And although we didn't have much money, I had clothes on my back, shoes on my feet and never wanted for food. We lived simple, but happy, never experiencing much loss or pain. All in all, my upbringing was ideal. After graduating high school, I went off to college, met and married a wonderful man, had two healthy babies, a boy and a girl, and lived in a nice house with my nice husband and nice life. Life was good!

Then, in 2006, the four of us moved from our small town of Durant, Oklahoma to the large metropolis of Oklahoma City so my husband, Joe, could attend Pharmacy school at the University of Oklahoma. We left all our family, friends and everything familiar when we moved. I found myself facing my first real struggle. Our children were very young at the time, 2 1/2 and 6 months, and I was home alone without a friend, without any family, and without much money. Much of Joe's days were filled with school and studying, leaving little time for family, much less any time for a job that could support us. We lived on student loans and the little money we had made from the sale of our home. I knew when we moved it would be a short-term sacrifice for our long-term betterment but still, I struggled with loneliness and feeling like Joe was moving forward, while I was being left behind. This was a new feeling for me. I had always felt fulfilled being a wife and mother, but I found in that time that I had to rely on God to strengthen me and give me purpose as I served my husband and children in that season.

Things improved, as we got involved in church. We attended Church of the Harvest and I made some friends, began serving in the children's ministry and found myself happier. Yet, I still felt restlessness in my heart, a longing for more, and a desire to have an impact beyond the four walls of my home. As pastors, my parents have given their lives to serve God and be in the ministry full time. They had been involved with missions my whole life but I never desired for it to be a part of mine. I never truly knew the need or desired to be a part of The Great Commission. That changed in February of 2007. Invited by some friends, Joe and I attended the annual Harvest Missions Banquet at our church to donate to the causes our church supported overseas. I didn't go expecting God to move on my heart beyond writing a donation check, but I ended up feeling completely compelled to do more than just give financially. That night, God called me to go to Cambodia. ME?! It was such an emotional moment for me. It was so scary for me to admit and then, commit to, because I had no idea where the money for the trip was going to come from. We were living on loans! But I stepped out in faith and obeyed. I believe that moment was one of the most defining moments of my life and looking back, I can see so many things have happened out of that moment!

God was so faithful and through the loving support of our family and friends, and even some people I hardly knew, the funds came in for the trip. In late July, my team and I traveled the 9,000 miles to Cambodia. To a nation where poverty dominates and hopelessness abounds. Still recovering from a destructive civil war in the 70's, Cambodia had become one of the leading countries of the sex-trade industry, exploiting young children and women due to its' extreme poverty and Godlessness. Mainly a Buddhist and superstitious culture, the love of God and His Gospel of hope and restoration hadn't been widespread.

While in Cambodia, our team worked alongside New Life Ministries (NLM) and Hagar House in Phnom Penh, the capital city of Cambodia. NLM, led by Pastor Jesse McCaul, an American from Oregon, has about 600+ members in over 60 churches throughout the provinces of Cambodia. Both ministries worked to bring hope, recovery and restoration to the destitute and exploited victims of poverty and injustice within their country. Their mission is to see lives rescued from the sex-trade industry and to give hope and purpose to the needy and poor. Through our partnership with them, we were able to practically show the love of God by serving at feeding centers where we fed the hungry and prayed over those who had need. We were given the opportunity to teach English and incorporate the Gospel to share the love of the Father and sow seeds of salvation with university students, some being Buddhist monks. We witnessed to shopkeepers when we bought supplies, and visited the slums where we prayed and handed out useful items to the needy. We led daytime church services for children who lived on the streets and washed and bandaged their dirty feet since many didn't have shoes. We traveled to the rural provinces to orphanages where we made improvements to facilities and ministered love to children with no families. We spent time with young girls, some as young as 3 and 4, who had been rescued from the sex trade industry and given shelter and safety and ultimately, hope and a chance to be children once again.

We served and gave and served some more, but the Lord supernaturally sustained us and opened our eyes to need, beyond what we could've imagined. He truly broke our heart for what breaks His! Yet, He also showed us the inextinguishable hope that is available in Him! It was incredible to meet those whose lives had been restored and witness firsthand the beauty Jesus can make out of ashes of brokenness and pain! Their faith wasn't one of complacency and lukewarm devotion, but sold-out abandon to the God that rescued them and a passion to share the hope they've found and reach the lost! That regardless of the poverty and hopelessness so prevalent around them, the Lord was at work in the hearts of people who had found the riches and joy of His love! It was beyond humbling to see! It impressed upon my heart, the joy I too can have when living with that kind of passion for the Lord each day!

I felt so alive during my time there and so grateful for my obedience to be led by the Holy Spirit and do something so outside of myself. I left with a greater heart of compassion and a greater desire to love the unloved, reach the lost and be God's hands and feet on the earth. I will be forever changed for the better for having gone to Cambodia! Looking back, I didn't know how this change in my heart would translate into my daily life, but I can see now how God was preparing my heart in a way I couldn't have imagined at the time.

After I came home, it took time to really process the emotions I experienced while I was away. Honestly, I felt convicted by my comfortable life. It's hard to not feel guilty when you've witnessed extreme poverty and loss. The Lord had to remind me not to judge and live condemned but to live thankful and willing to serve and give wherever He calls us. He moved in small ways at times, and in large ways in others. I knew God was leading me and wanted to use my mother's heart to reach children specifically. So I got involved with a foster care ministry that sponsored a Christmas party in December and a free summer camp for foster children ages 7-12 in June. Royal Family Kids Camp is one of the most amazing camps I believe there is! It's provided absolutely free and is five days of lavishing God's love on children who have been abused and abandoned! The children I met during my years of volunteering had many different stories, but all shared the common thread of confusion, hurt and lack of worth. It was amazing the transformation in their little spirits after five days of constant love, attention, prayer and being fed God's Word! I knew that besides being a mama to my two babies, God was calling me to "mother" and love these broken hearts and show them the Love of their Heavenly Father! I was heartbroken to leave that ministry behind when called to move back to Durant after my father-in-law's passing and Joe's graduation from pharmacy school. Nothing like that existed in Durant.

In late May of 2010, we moved home and settled into our new, yet familiar, life. But, my little babies were babies no more. Noah was entering first grade and our youngest daughter Maya, was about to start pre-K. I knew I was called to stay home and raise my children, but they were both school age. What now? Get a job? I wanted to always be available for my kids and since Joe was working as a Pharmacist and made a good living, it wasn't necessary to get by. So I continued to stay home and eventually we got a dog! Major was my companion during the day and he and the Lord helped ease the loneliness I felt in our quiet house. I stayed busy volunteering at the kid's school and in a local clothing bank ministry. I made fellow stay-at-home mom friends and eventually really began to enjoy my day-to-day freedom.

I was happy with my life and didn't anticipate changing it up any time soon. But in March of 2013, we lost our dog in a tragic accident. We were crushed.

Me especially. I had a good friend call me one day and tell me that in her prayer time, when praying for us, she felt the Lord impress upon her heart that He would bring us a greater blessing than the one we lost. He would restore our broken hearts and balm it with more love than we could've known. At the time, we both were assuming another furry friend!

But around that same time, we got a call from a family member that was expecting a baby. She called with a medicine question for Joe, but then began to share the challenges she was having as a soon to be single mother and the fear that she would be unable to keep the baby. A few weeks later, Joe felt impressed to call and check on her. Once again, conversation turned to her fear that the baby would end up in foster care. Joe had gone into our bedroom for privacy and I distinctly remember walking in and overhearing him say, "Hannah has worked with foster care and if your system is anything like Oklahoma's, it's full of issues and problems. I would hate for the baby to end up there so I want you to know that Hannah and I will take the baby if it comes down to that." I stopped dead in my tracks! What in the world was he saying?! We hadn't even remotely discussed anything about taking a baby! After he hung up, I immediately told him no way! A baby? Our children were 9 and 7! Perfect age! They were self sufficient and independent and I liked it that way! A baby? I couldn't even imagine going back to bottles and diapers! Joe just asked me to please think about it.

Months passed and the baby was born. He came several weeks early and needed to be placed in the neonatal intensive care unit for complications. Like his mother feared, the baby, a tiny blue-eyed boy named Wyatt, was placed in the state's foster system. Joe still felt certain we should take him, but I wavered. It wasn't until Joe shared with me how he was so certain this was what God wanted us to do, that my spirit responded to the call. He felt that in us taking Wyatt, and bringing him into our family, that we were placing him under a new covenant of blessing and lineage of Godliness that would restore in his heart a brokenness that plagued a part of our family. Having had the best dad in the world, a man that exemplified Jesus, Joe knew the importance of having a Godly man to guide, teach and believe in you. He felt God was calling him to do what his dad had done, and lovingly model being what a real man is, to Wyatt. My spirit leapt at his words and immediately, my heart was changed! Later, during my prayer time, the Lord brought to my remembrance 1 John 3:16-19. It says, *"This is how we know what love is: Jesus Christ laid down his life for us. And we ought to lay down our lives for our brothers. If anyone has material possessions and sees his brother in need, but has no pity on him, how can the love of God be in him? Dear Children, let us not love with words alone, but with action and in truth."* Hadn't God already called me to compassion? Hadn't He broken my heart for the broken and given me a passion for the fatherless, specifically those in foster care? My testimony was beginning to come full circle. God was revealing to me that instead of a new puppy to love or a camp to serve a week at, He was calling for a greater commitment; us to parent a baby, full of need and care, to bless and guide who, in turn, would be a blessing and lifelong source of love for us! What an amazing journey it was to that point!

We quickly began working toward becoming a licensed foster home so Wyatt could be transferred to our care while we worked towards adoption. It was almost immediately that opposition came from all sides and we began to be under a full-fledged spiritual attack. It was very clear the enemy was against God's plan for this boy and that there was great spiritual significance in what we were doing. I was hit emotionally through conflict with an acquaintance that really hurt me. I didn't have problems with people! I'm easy to get along with and work at being a peacemaker so I was stunned! Then we were hit financially over and over, where we had previously seemed to operate under an umbrella of favor and divine provision. It was absurd! We got audited by the IRS, Joe was promised a bonus that ended up falling through, we had bills come due that we didn't expect and were forced to sell Joe's nice truck for something more affordable. Some days were very discouraging, but we kept our resolve, knowing what God called us to do.

We met little Wyatt, two months old at the time, in June of 2013. We knew right away he was meant to be a part of our family. It was such a bonding time! We were also able to spend time with his birth mom and more extended family and found such peace in knowing they all supported us and wanted us to raise him. Having their blessing meant the world to us! Our older children were unable to come that visit, but loved him already even though they had seen him only in pictures. It was amazing! It took a few more months and lots of prayers, tears and even a call to our local Senator before all the paperwork was filed and complete and we were cleared to bring Wyatt home.

On September 20th, 2013, we walked into our home at 1529 Remington West Circle, having left being a family of four, but returning as an official family of five! Noah and Maya were overwhelmed with love for their new little brother and have to this day, not stopped doting on him! Wyatt's official adoption was filed on November 4th, 2014, our oldest son, Noah's 11th birthday. We thank God for the honor to love and raise our son, Wyatt, and are beyond amazed at the supernatural heart connection we have to him! We truly love him like he was born of us, just like Noah and Maya! It hasn't been easy transitioning to having a baby again, but its drawn me closer to the Lord still and made me realize that God's plan is so much bigger than I could ever imagine! My testimony is probably just beginning.

God Provided the
Answer in a Dream

By: Susan Dodson

"And it shall come to pass in the last days, says God, That I will pour out of My Spirit on all flesh; Your sons and your daughters shall prophesy, Your young men shall see visions, Your old men shall dream dreams.

Acts 2:17

*R*andy Dodson was a good man who trusted God above everything else. From the time he could talk, all he ever wanted to be was a cowboy. He loved to be outdoors and see the sun rise and he liked being outside when the sun went down. He was a simple man in many ways, in that he loved his Father, his family and his church in that order and loved living in the country and being around cattle and horses and dogs.

Randy had worked for United Parcel Service for 10 years and was very happy when he had saved enough to lease some land and make a living raising cattle. He was always thinking of how to "fine-tune" his cattle operation and make it more profitable. He studied feed rations, changed bulls, and improved his pastures in order to sell bigger calves in the fall.

One year he decided that he and his wife, Sue, should take their hay barn and turn it into a place to make feed. He told Sue one day as they were out on their feed route that if they could sell at least 2 tons of special mixed feed a day they could pay for what they were feeding their herd. Sue's pessimistic response was, "Randy, we will never sell two tons a day!" Her thoughts were based on the fact that they lived 3 miles out of town and a quarter of a mile off the highway and the town only had a population of 750 and most didn't have cattle.

But Randy was adamant and they started by setting up some grain bins where they could take full truckloads of corn and alfalfa. They borrowed one of their neighbor's bins to hold soybean meal. It was a mile and a half down the road. They started mixing the grain in a mixer/grinder ran by the tractor and would sack it by hand and tie the tops with string. Each sack was weighed on a scale and adjusted by hand. It was a cumbersome process that involved Randy, Sue, and their children, but served the purpose for a month or two. Then as word spread of the good quality feed that was available locally other ranchers came wanting to buy also.

Randy and Sue were such novices that they had no clue as to what was available for handling feed, etc. They eventually bought a handheld sewing machine that would sew the tops of sacks but it was still a slow process that wasn't keeping up with the demand. Sue asked Randy what they were going to do since there were not enough hours in the day to meet the workload. Randy, in his usual calm manner, said he didn't know yet.

Randy was the music minister for the local interdenominational church and was a mentor to many young men in the church. On many occasions when asked for his opinion on how to solve problems, he would say, "When something is bothering me, I just pray about it before I go to bed and I ask God to show me the answer in a dream. When I wake up, I'll have the answer." Those young men would laugh and say that this probably meant that he was an "old man" because young men see visions! His reply was a steady, "Then do whatever works for you and God."

One morning, when Sue woke up, Randy was sitting on the side of the bed with "eyes as big as saucers". She at first was alarmed and sensed that something was wrong. She said, "Randy, what's going on?" His reply was, "God showed me in a dream how to build a feed sacker." Sue sensed that Randy had had a real encounter with God and was excited to see what was going to happen next.

Randy didn't waste any time and phoned a long time friend who was a welder. He asked him to come out and spend a couple days with him on a welding project he needed done. Randy told Duke what metal he would need and had him order it for him. When Duke questioned Randy about what they were going to be building, Randy was evasive and told him he would show him when he arrived.

Duke was a very good, hard-working man who didn't go to church and didn't want to discuss religion. When he arrived in a couple of days with his welder and the metal, the work started. Randy never wrote anything down, but would draw off sections to explain to Duke what he wanted as the welding started. At a certain point when they had stopped for a break, Randy shared with Duke what the Lord had shown him in a dream. Duke was quiet for a moment and then said, "Well let's get back to it." The work went on for a couple of days and then the final weld was completed. Randy, Sue and Duke stood back to look at this giant metal hopper with trapdoors, catching bin, levers and counterweights and were amazed at what they had built from God's blueprint. Now the only question was whether it would work or not.

They backed the tractor and grinder into the barn, filled it half full of grain and attached a sack to the bottom of the sacker. When they pulled the lever to let the grain fall into the smaller bin, it steadily filled the smaller bin until it reached a certain weight and then it automatically shut off. Sue and Duke were standing there awestruck by the fact that it had worked perfectly on the first attempt. Randy had a look of, "I knew it would work from the moment I opened my eyes from the dream that God gave me!" There was a lot of celebrating that happened that day with Randy and Sue and a lot of head shaking from Duke who couldn't believe that a dream had produced this piece of equipment that would sack feed without any electricity or power and was only based on counterweights and levers. Isn't God amazing in His wisdom and concern about our everyday problems?

Randy went on to establish a successful feed business that brought people from as far as Fort Worth, Texas and produced the feed that fed the Grand Champion Steer at the Houston Livestock Show one year. Randy was quick to remind Sue of the comment she had made years before about her doubts that they would ever sell 2 tons of feed in a day, on a day that they sold 110 tons in one day. God is faithful and present in our daily lives.

The Gift of Healing

By: Lena B. Earles

One of my greatest blessings from the Lord came in 1965, when I found a lump under my left arm. It was so sore I couldn't lie on my side at night. I prayed for healing, but it didn't happen.

One Sunday, my family went to Oklahoma City to visit my parents. We spent the entire day together and went to church with them that night. At the end of the service, the pastor asked for anyone who needed prayer for healing to come forward. I considered going, but decided not to since I was a visitor. I was standing there thinking about what I should do when I heard a voice behind me say, "This is your time." We were sitting on the back row. I turned to see who had spoken, but there was no one there. I turned to my husband, but he had heard nothing. I thought it must be the Lord speaking to me. I stepped out into the aisle and was healed before I reached the pastor. The soreness was gone instantly and the lump disappeared.

On March 29, 2001, I went to the doctor for my yearly checkup. Everything was fine. On April 15, Easter Sunday morning, I found a lump under my right arm while taking a shower. I went back to the doctor again for another mammogram. Nothing showed up, but the doctor sent me to a surgeon to remove the lump. Four lymph nodes had grown together, and it was cancer. I was sent to the OU Institute Breast Care Center for an ultrasound and a biopsy. Two cancers were found in my right breast. I went back to the surgeon and had both breasts removed, along with all the lymph nodes from the right side. I had cancer in fourteen lymph nodes and the doctors were not sure where the primary cancer was. Things were not going well for me, so my children thought I should go to M.D. Anderson in Houston, Texas.

My daughter, Alicia, called the hospital several times a day until they assigned me a doctor. My first appointment was with Dr. Margorie Green on July 31. She was a critical care doctor. My cancer was called Ductal Carcinoma, stage four.

One of God's blessings came when Alicia ran into a doctor friend in Oklahoma City. She told him of my condition and that I would be going to Houston for my treatments. He insisted that Angel Flight would fly me. A pilot would pick me up in Hinton, where I lived and would return me there. All flights were grounded after 9/11, but they got special permission for that flight.

Another blessing: I was on a three-day chemotherapy treatment with four kinds of chemo, and I never vomited. There were days when I didn't feel well and was very weak and tired, but I did much better than most of the other patients being treated.

Another blessing: After the chemotherapy, I would have to stay in Houston for the radiation treatments and would need an apartment for about two months. A hurricane had just come through the Gulf and most of the apartments for cancer patients had been flooded and could not be occupied. One day, I was in my hotel room and the phone rang. When I answered, a man asked, "Do you need an apartment?" I answered in the affirmative and he gave me an address. We went to see it and could not believe how nice it was. It was located in the back of a Lutheran church. Everything was furnished, including a washer and dryer. All we had to supply was our food.

My radiation treatments were not easy. I got five zaps a day. They were so strong and burned me so badly that my skin just sloughed off. I was kept with my critical care doctor for six years and transferred to an oncologist for a yearly checkup. I have had almost thirteen years of good health since I finished my treatments.

I am so thankful to the Lord for restoring my health, but my greatest blessing of all was when the Lord saved me.

The Whisper of His Name Changes Everything

By: Sherry Holeman

One early spring morning, I was getting ready to go outside to feed our chickens when our daughter, Laura, ran into the kitchen and asked me if she could help gather the eggs. Laura was only three years old at the time and caring for animals was quite an enjoyment for her. She would carry our egg basket and count the eggs as we put them into the basket. After we gathered the eggs, we would water the flowers with our well water. I had told Laura often not to drink the water because we had never had it tested to see if it was safe to drink. I told her the well water was for watering our yard and flowers only and if she ever wanted to drink some water that our drinking water came out of the faucet in the kitchen. We watered the flowers and then Laura asked if she could go to our neighbor's house.

Our neighbor, Tanya Smalling, had five-year-old twin boys and Laura loved to play with them. Laura asked me if she could go over to their house for a while, so I called Tanya to see if Laura could play with the twins. Tanya said, "Sure, bring her over." Laura had been at Tanya's for a few hours when my phone rang. It was Tanya on the line saying that she thought Laura was sick. She said she started throwing up and didn't feel well, so I went over and got her. The twins hadn't been sick, so it wasn't anything she picked up from them; I figured she just ate something that upset her tummy and after a few hours she would be fine.

I bought her home and put her to bed and she continued to throw up. Everything I gave her from water to popsicles came up. My mom taught me years ago that before you call the doctor, you call on the Lord. So I laid my hand on her tummy and began to pray that He would heal her little body. As the hours passed by, Laura got worse. Her tummy would make awful groaning noises then she would grab her tummy, scream, and cry to make it stop. I rushed her into the bathroom because I knew with any viral bug she would probably have diarrhea along with vomiting. Sure enough, she did have diarrhea but it was more than that, she was hemorrhaging. I called Randy, my husband, at work and told him Laura was really sick and was passing blood and I didn't know what to do. Randy was much calmer than I was in circumstances like this. He thought it was probably nothing serious. He said to call him back if she didn't get better. A little later I called him back and told him to come home as soon as possible and to pick me up some diapers to put on Laura. Laura was potty-trained, but because she was passing lots of blood so often, I needed diapers. I told Randy we needed to get her to the doctor. He came home with diapers, so I put one on Laura. Randy held her in his arms and began to love on her. Her daddy always could make her feel better. Randy saw how sick she was and listened to her agonizing cries when she had stomach cramps, and he agreed with me that she needed to see a doctor.

When we got her to the doctor's office, they said it was probably just a virus and that she would be fine after 24 hours. The doctor gave her a prescription for the vomiting and diarrhea and told us to take her home and let her sleep. We took her home, gave her the medicine the doctor prescribed and put her to bed. I sat by her bed while she slept because I was afraid to leave her side. A mama seems to know when something isn't right with her children and in my gut I felt this was something serious, so I needed to stay close by her.

A few hours went by as Laura finally began to sleep a little. She would wake up from time to time through the night when I had to change her diapers. I decided it was important to know how often she was hemorrhaging, so I began to keep count of the diaper changes. The pain she was in must have been horrific because she would scream the worst screams as her tummy made horrible noises. I would scream and cry for God to heal her with each scream I heard. Fear gripped my heart every time I changed her diapers. I couldn't understand why God had not already healed her. Why hasn't He heard my prayers? I began to question God even though I knew in my heart that His ways are not always understandable. The pain seemed to let up for a while, so I drifted back to sleep. When I awoke Laura was lifeless. She had turned so pale and her head hung over my arms as I picked her up. I ran and woke up Randy and told him we had to get to the hospital with Laura because something was wrong with her. Her breathing was very shallow. When I picked her up, she just lay in my arms and wouldn't lift her head when I spoke to her. I had gone through a large box of diapers by morning, so I knew something was definitely wrong.

We rushed her to the local hospital to see if they could help her. When we arrived at the emergency room, Randy filled out the paperwork as I held Laura, praying that God would heal her body. Finally, we were taken to a private room. I didn't know the doctor on call early that morning, but he seemed to be concerned about her. He ordered the nurse to start an IV to give her some fluids. They called Laura's doctor and he arrived to examine her. He told us he would start running some lab work on her, but that he felt like she was extremely dehydrated because of the loss of fluid in her body. He told us he would give her a couple bags of fluid and she would be fine. The nurse put an IV in her little arm and began to get the fluid started.

A few hours went by and the nurse changed the IV bag out but Laura wasn't showing any signs of improvement. Her doctor was scheduled to go to an out of town conference that weekend, but he seemed very concerned about Laura. He said," By now, I thought I would have seen some improvement. I'm going to cancel my trip and watch her closely." I'm so thankful we had a caring doctor. He asked me if we had any chickens and if Laura had been around them that the morning. I told him she loved to help gather the eggs in the morning, but she never picked up the eggs. She would just hold the basket and count the eggs as we gathered them. I told him we had well water that we do not drink, but she may have taken a drink of it from the hose without my noticing. He said he would run lab work to see if it was a Roto virus, Salmonella, E-coli, or something caused by the water. We thanked him for his concern.

The first day in the hospital seemed very long. We called home to the boys and told them we would be at the hospital for a while to try to get Laura well. Our two boys were 10 and 12 years older than their sister. When our lives were blessed with Laura, her brothers treated her like a little princess. They say we spoiled her, but they did their fair share as well. They loved their little sister so much and they wanted to see her well again. The boys stayed with our neighbor, Tanya, while we were at the hospital.

The days at the hospital seemed to get longer. Laura was not getting any better. In 24 hours she had gone through 66 diapers. I knew my baby was terribly sick and I didn't know what to do about it. Three days went by with no signs of improvement. On the third morning, the doctor came into her room and told us he was still waiting on some more lab work, but everything he had tested her for was negative. He wasn't sure what was wrong with her and didn't know why she was not improving. He would continue to run more tests and would check on her later.

Laura had completely lost her appetite. She would only sip on water because we insisted she drink something. She would look at me with sad eyes and say, "Mommy, make me better." I held her little hand and said, "I'm really trying to, baby. The doctor is trying to help us make you better. God's going to heal you real soon." As soon as I said those words, I would question God again. "Why are you not listening to me, God? Why don't you heal my baby?" What if God didn't heal her, am I ready to release her to Him should she die? So many questions went through my mind. I had to trust her to God's care no matter what the outcome.

Our parents had been calling to check on her as well. My mama was a prayer warrior and I knew she was praying for Laura. We were bombarding heaven with our prayers for her. God seem to be silent though for now because nothing was changing for Laura. She had been in the hospital since Tuesday, with no improvement. It was Friday and still no change. Laura had also lost a lot of weight. The doctor ran numerous tests in search of how to treat the infection, but every test came back negative. I knew God must have something special for Laura to do in life because Satan was trying to steal our baby from us.

Our parents decided to come in for the weekend to see her. My parents came by the hospital for a while to visit her on Saturday, and then Randy's mom and dad visited later that day. Our parents were just as concerned as we were. They knew something wasn't right when they saw her little sick body.

By Sunday, we still had not seen any improvement. Randy and I were extremely exhausted. Randy was trying to stay calm for me because he knows how I worry. I could tell from his eyes that he was worried too. Randy stayed positive, though, throughout the whole ordeal. He is my rock when times get tough. He always reminds me to put my faith in action and believe God is working even though we don't always see what He's doing. He reminded me that God always comes through for us and He will come through again. I'm so thankful God has blessed me with a wonderful husband and a loving father to our children. He is always there when we need him, just like God is always there when we need our Heavenly Father because that's what dads do.

That Sunday afternoon, my parents stayed for a while and then they had to leave to go home. Mama held Laura and prayed for her and then she held me in her arms before she left and tried to assure me everything would be ok. She was praying and believing God for a miracle to take place. Later that afternoon, Randy's parents visited for a while and held Laura. While they were visiting us, Laura had drifted off to sleep. My parents had just left and around 3 o'clock my in-laws decided to leave. My parents lived in Anadarko, Oklahoma and Randy's lived in McAlester. Both of them had a ways to travel.

Laura had been sleeping awhile when the chaplain for the day came into her room. He was a Pentecostal minister from one of the local churches. He asked if he could pray with Laura. We told him we would appreciate the prayers. I had visited his church during revivals from time to time, so I knew he was a rather loud minister when he prayed. Laura's arms were bruised from all the needles. She had been poked and prodded so much that week from nurses drawing blood and changing out her IV bag. Her veins were like mine, very deep and small. Her veins had blown a few times so the nurses had to change positions of her IV a few times as well. She was so badly bruised and at times very frightened when people touched her. She was still sleeping when the chaplain laid his hand on her head and began to pray. As he prayed, he began to shake her head. The more he prayed, the louder he got. Laura woke up from the noise and started screaming, "Mommy, Mommy. Make him stop!" She was not aware of what was happening to her. I don't have a problem with ministers praying for my children, but that Sunday I became very distraught with the chaplain. Laura was so frustrated and looking at me to help her. I was exhausted and full of fear, and I suppose I let my exasperation and exhaustion get the best of me. I am ashamed to say this, but I thanked the chaplain for praying and asked him to leave because he had frightened my child.

Randy tried to calm me down and told me it was not the chaplain's fault that Laura was sick. He apologized to the chaplain and told him more about what had happened to Laura. The chaplain apologized for scaring her and waking her up. Randy's parents decided they had better go home before it got any later, so I stayed with Laura while Randy walked them out to their car. When Randy got back I was still complaining about the chaplain. Laura was still screaming and crying, and I had started crying telling him I didn't know why God wasn't healing our baby. Randy had his hands full with both Laura and me having a fit. Randy told me to control myself. He told me to go to the chapel at the end of the hall and spend some quiet time with God because my emotions were making things worse. He took Laura from my arms to try to calm her down. I left the room to go to the chapel, but before I went to the chapel I went to the nurses station on Laura's floor and turned in a complaint about the chaplain. I complained about him shaking her head and scaring her. I then went to the chapel to pray. I sat down and bowed my head in silence. I began to sob, not knowing the future of our baby. Was He going to spare her life as He had mine years ago in a car accident or was He going to let her die? Only God has the answers to my questions. I then asked God to forgive me for being so upset at the chaplain. I asked God to give me direction and answers. I saw a Bible on the table by the couch. I normally know where I want to read when I do my Bible reading, but that day I didn't know where to read. I was so full of emotions and was looking at the storm we were in that I felt completely numb. I wanted answers, but where were they? I couldn't remember where all the healing scriptures were in the Bible; scriptures that I had memorized when I was a young child. Mama taught me to memorize the Bible when I was young. Where was the scripture about Jesus being wounded for our transgressions and bruised for our iniquities? I knew it was in Isaiah somewhere, but where? I picked up the Bible and asked God to show me where to read. I opened the Bible and it fell open to 1 Kings 19:1–13. The prophet Elijah had been running from a wicked woman named Jezebel. He was fearful for his life. He had fallen asleep when an angel touched him and told him to get up and eat; so he ate. He cooked the bread that the angel had left him. The angel came a second time and told him to get up and eat, so he again obeyed the Lord. He journeyed on for 40 days and 40 nights until he reached Horeb, the mountain of God. He went into a cave and slept for the night. The Lord woke him and asked him what he was doing? Elijah told Him that he was zealous for God Almighty. He told God that all the prophets had been to put to death by the sword and he was next. God told him to go out and stand on the mountain in the presence of the Lord, for the Lord was getting ready to pass by. Then a great and powerful wind tore the mountains apart and shattered the rocks before the Lord, but the Lord was not in the earthquake. After the earthquake, came a fire, but the Lord wasn't in the fire. After the fire came a gentle whisper. When Elijah heard it he covered his face for God was in the whisper. Suddenly, after reading that God wasn't in the wind or the fire, but was in the whisper, I began to cry out to God in a whisper. A blanket of peace engulfed me and I knew God was trying to speak to me. I cried out to God and said, "Lord, just the whisper of your name, Jesus, and my baby will be made whole." I began to sing a song I learned years ago called "The Whisper of His Name" and I asked God to please bring Laura healing in a whisper. I now had an unexplainable peace in my heart that Laura was going to be okay. I thanked God for speaking to me through His word and I closed the Bible to head back to Laura's room.

As I was walking down the hall, I saw the chaplain coming out of her room again so I frantically hurried inside. As I entered the room, I saw her daddy holding her. She was so peaceful in his arms just as we are in God's arms when he brings us assurance all will be ok. I asked Randy with disgust in my voice if that was the chaplain that had upset Laura. Randy calmed me down and told me that the chaplain came back because he heard Laura screaming and crying when he left. He was concerned that he had upset her. He asked Randy if he could whisper a prayer over her. Randy said you could barely hear his voice. He so silently whispered the name of Jesus over and over. He never laid his hand on her. He just stood over her, prayed and whispered the name of Jesus. She quieted down so quickly as he whispered a prayer over her. I was amazed at what Randy had told me. I had just asked God to come in a whisper and heal our baby. God heard my prayer. I told Randy about what I read while in the chapel. Randy gently put Laura back in bed so she could rest. It had been a long day and we both sat down and drifted off to sleep.

Around 6 PM, the nurses brought Randy and I food trays for our evening meal. They had been so kind to us while we were there with Laura. They knew we were worried parents and wouldn't leave her side. We thanked them for the meal and began to eat. I had just told Randy how I wished Laura was well. As we were eating, Laura woke up. She loved chicken and rice and that was the meal for the night. She hadn't eaten anything for about 6 days because she couldn't keep the food down without vomiting. She looked at me and smiled. Her countenance had changed so much that evening. I smiled back at her and said, "Mommy and Daddy are here." She said, "Mommy, I'm hungry. Can I have some chicken and rice too?" I was so excited that she actually wanted to eat. She seemed to have some energy that we hadn't seen in days. I told Randy I was going to ask the nurse if I could share my food with her. Randy stayed by Laura's side telling her we were going to see if she could eat. I ran to the nurses' station and asked if I could give Laura some of our food because she was finally hungry. The nurse called the doctor and asked if he could have some chicken and rice. The doctor told them to bring her a tray and let her eat all she wants. The nurse had a food tray brought up to her room. When Laura saw the food, her eyes got so big. She ate the chicken and rice, mashed potatoes, green beans, cherry Jell-O, and cookie and drank all the carton of milk. After she ate her food, she asked her daddy to play "Ring around the Rosie". He was so excited to see the change that yes, you guessed it, they were playing "Ring around the Rosie". Randy would push around her IV pole while she ran in circles. She asked her daddy to play "hide and seek", and he played one game after another with her. It seemed as if she was a big ball of energy. I knew now that something had changed. The whisper of God had touched our baby. The whisper of His name had changed everything. Later that evening, the hemorrhaging began to let up. The Son had come over the horizon of the storm and the calmness had been restored. We had made it to the other side. I knew God had spoken to the winds and waves in our lives and calmed the storm for us through the whisper of His name.

The next morning the doctor came by to check on Laura. She had improved tremendously. He said he didn't know what kind of illness she had because all the test performed on her ended up being negative. He said if she still showed signs of improvement she would be able to go home later that evening. We brought her home that night. She was still passing some blood but with every diaper I thanked God for His healing touch. Another week went by and all the bleeding stopped. God had truly healed our little Laura.

We never found out what illness Laura had. I believe Satan was trying to destroy her because he knew she had a call of God on her life. Laura is now 17 years old, and at a young age received the Lord as her Savior was filled with the Holy Ghost not long after she was saved. At the age of 10, she began to sing songs to God. God has blessed Laura with a beautiful voice. Laura told us at the age of 15 that God called her to go into youth ministry. Laura will graduate from high school next year and is seeking God's direction as to where she needs to go to college and prepare herself for His ministry. I am so thankful for God's healing in her life and the talents God has bestowed on her. I truly know that one whisper of the name of Jesus changes everything. I have seen it in our own lives.

My Testimony of the Miracle-Working Power of God

By: Sherrie Holeman

I am the daughter of Billy and Thayla Graham. My parents had five children-all girls. Glenda was ten years older than me, my sister Janice was eight years older, Joyce was three years older, and then Mom gave birth to me. Mom said that when I was born she cried because I wasn't a boy. She just knew after three girls God was going to give her a son, so when she found out she had given birth to another girl, she was very disappointed. Her mother scolded her and told her that God gives and takes away so she needed to be thankful for His gift of another girl and remember that God knows what we need when we need it. My dad had a twin sister named Betty Jean whom he lost to rheumatic fever at the age of 16. My sister, Joyce Dean, was named after my dad so my parents decided to name me "Sherry Jean" after his twin sister. Four years after I was born my mom gave birth to another girl. Dad decided to name her Tommy since he never got a son.

Dad was a farmer and spent many Sundays in the fields preparing the land for planting or harvesting crops. Dad was a Christian in his younger years, but as he grew older he made caring for the farm and family his first priority and drifted away from God.

My mom had been praying, "Lord, do whatever it takes to bring Bill back to you. Help him see that if he doesn't surrender to you, he will be lost for eternity."

One night around the middle of November 1969, Mom had a bad dream that I was hit and killed by a semi-truck. She woke up alarmed and became fearful that something was going to happen to me. My dad's mother had died in October and Mom felt that another death in the family so soon would be more than our family could handle, so she began to pray for my protection. After a few days went by and nothing happened, Mom decided that it must have just been a bad dream and had no meaning. Two weeks later on Saturday, November 29, 1969, in the afternoon I became very tired and told Mom I was going to take a nap. She told me she would wake me up in time to eat supper. I went to bed and as I slept, a dream came to me. I saw my bed turn to gold and four angels came around me. One angel was on the right side of the bed and the other on the left side of the bed, another at the head of the bed and the other at the foot of the bed. They joined together around me and carried me in their arms to heaven. Then I awoke from the dream. It was so beautiful and brought such excitement to me that I ran in the kitchen where Mom was and told her about the angels carrying me to heaven. Mom sat down and began to wring her hands over and over in the apron she was wearing. I could see a look of worry on her face. Mom told me years later that my dream made her remember her dream about me being killed. She felt as if both dreams were a sign from God that something was definitely going to happen to me, but God was going to take care of me.

My sister, Janice, was in high school and had been witnessing to a school classmate, Walter, because he didn't believe that God was real. She asked Walter what God would have to do in order for him to believe that God was real. Walter told her that if God was real, He would have to come down and perform a miracle before his eyes and then he would believe. Janice told him that God loved him so much and that if performing a miracle before him would make him believe, then God might just do that very thing in order to prove His love to him.

Later, Dad hired Walter to work at our farm on the weekends. It was cotton season, so Dad was trying to get the cotton harvested before the weather turned bad. He asked Walter to be at the farm early Sunday morning so they could get an early start. I was seven-and- a-half years old and had just started the second grade at Bray Elementary School. I loved school, as well as, Sunday school. Even though Dad was not attending church regularly, Mom was still very faithful to church. Mom was my Sunday school teacher and very rarely missed a Sunday service. Sunday, November 30, 1969 was different.

I had just finished getting ready for church and was sitting in the living room waiting on Mom to finish getting my little sister and herself ready so we could leave for church. Dad had sent word to Mom that he needed her to make him a jug of water and have one of us girls bring it to him before we left for church. My sister, Glenda, filled the water cooler with ice water. She asked Mom if she could send me outside to give the water to Walter and let him take it to Dad since she was still getting ready for church. Glenda and Mom had no idea that Dad and Walter were no longer in our yard, but were now across the highway in the cotton field.

Our farm was in a valley on highway 19, sixteen miles east of Marlow, Oklahoma. I went outside to give Daddy the water jug, but by now he was already on the tractor across the highway from our house. I went across the road and gave the jug of water to Walter and asked him to give it to Daddy. He told me to be careful going home. I left the field and headed across the road to go back home so we could go to church. I'm not sure why, but for some reason I hesitated and stopped in the road.

An elderly lady traveling from west to east saw me standing in the road and tried to stop to avoid hitting me. She slammed on her brakes, which caused her car to go into a whirlwind spin and the corner of her bumper hit me in the head and hurled me 75 feet through the air. When I came down, the top of my skull hit the highway. Dad said when he heard her brakes, he ran with Walter to see if I was alive. Dad said when he got to me, I looked like a mangled up piece of cotton. Blood was everywhere; my eyes were rolled back in my head. I had lacerations and was not responsive. He picked me up in his arms and began to pray over me. He swore to God if He would spare my life and allow me to live, he would surrender his life to Him and get back in church.

Mom ran outside the minute she heard the commotion; she knew what had taken place. The dream she feared had now happened. Thoughts ran through her mind as her dream flashed before her. Is she alive? If she is alive, will she be normal again? So many thoughts raced through her mind.

A stranger who had a new white car stopped to help and told my dad to load me in his car and they would get me to the nearest hospital since he could get there quicker than an ambulance could. Dad told him that his car would be ruined, but the stranger wouldn't take no for an answer and insisted that Dad and I get into the car. They took me to the Marlow hospital. As they were in transport, Dad said he had to straighten up all of my teeth. He said my teeth were twisted and knocked loose, so to keep them from falling out of my mouth, he straightened them up and held them in place with his hands until we got to the hospital.

When we arrived at the hospital, the doctor told my parents that I had a concussion, broken bones throughout my body, a collapsed chest cavity, and a cerebral hematoma. I was also in a coma. The doctor said that I had gravel in my skull and that I had swallowed a lot of gravel that they were able to get out of me. He told my parents that it would be a miracle if I survived and, if that were the case, I would most likely be an invalid. Mom told the doctor that God doesn't start something and not finish it. She trusted God to take care of me.

I was put in an ambulance and transported to St. Anthony's Children's Hospital in Oklahoma City. Mom said on her way to St. Anthony's she remembered crying the day I was born because she had given birth to another girl and how my grandma had told her that God give and He takes away and God could take me away as fast as I was given. Mom asked for God's forgiveness and asked Him to restore me completely and not leave me an invalid. She prayed and rededicated me to God and asked the Lord to allow His perfect will to be done in my life. She said, "God, if you choose to take her life, then give me the grace to accept it, but if you choose to allow her to live, then please restore her body, mind, and spirit completely. I promise to raise her to serve you all the days of her life if you will allow her to live."

My family had contacted prayer warriors in our church and asked them to start a prayer chain for my healing. People began to spread the word that we needed a miracle from God to spare my life. Churches from all over began to pray for me. Mom said even missionaries received word that we needed prayer. So many prayers were being offered up to God for me from everywhere.

Mom said when we arrived at St. Anthony's Hospital, the ER doctors looked at the x-rays that my doctor sent with the EMS from the Marlow Hospital and examined me again. The doctors told Mom and Dad that I was a miracle. They said that when they examined me, my chest cavity was no longer collapsed and I had no broken bones whatsoever, yet there was scar tissue throughout my body as though I had been in a body cast or had surgery. The doctors confirmed that I had a cerebral hematoma and was in a coma and the next 24-48 hours were going to be critical. There was no certainty that I would live.

My dad began to fast and pray along with my mom for my healing. I was in a deep coma for 10 days. One morning when my parents came to my room, I was awake and sitting up with a blank stare on my face. They began to talk to me but I would not respond. Mom asked the nurse why I wouldn't talk to them. The nurse said that I was in a semi-comatose state and I may never come out of it. Mom said it was as though I was in a world of my own. She said one day I was coloring a picture when she arrived, so she began to talk to me telling me how much she loved me, but it seemed as though I was alone in the room because I never reacted to anyone who spoke to me.

The doctors told my parents that most likely I would never be able to walk, talk or function as a normal human being again because of the damaged brain cells. Mom told the doctor that she served a God who could do anything and nothing was too hard for Him. She called our pastor at Pearl Assembly of God Church and asked him to please have our church family continue to pray for complete healing in my body. Mom said I stayed in this mental and physical condition for another 10 days.

I was released from the hospital, but was in occupational, speech, and physical therapy for 6 years. Mom never let me be a quitter. She would hold my face in her hands when things were tough for me and tell me that "CAN" lives here. She said God is not a liar. His Words are true for in Philippians 4:13 He says, "I can do ALL things through Christ who strengthens me." That scripture became my strength. Mom put it everywhere in my room and made me learn to say it over and over again. She made me memorize scriptures and would not allow me to give up. She would not do things for me, but made me do them myself. The doctor had told her it was important to push me to do things for myself in order for me to function again.

Mom said when I was able to talk, I told them about my nurse, Tammy. She wore a beautiful white gown and had beautiful white hair and the voice of an angel. She colored with me, sang to me, bathed me, brushed my hair, and read to me. Mom asked the nurses if she could meet her so she could thank her. The nurses said I had never had a nurse named Tammy and no one looked like what I had described. Mama said she felt as if it must have been my guardian angel taking care of me. I talked to Mama about her all the time when I was growing up. My granny had died before the accident and Mama said I told her that Granny kept telling me I couldn't stay with her, but had to go back home.

While I was in St. Anthony's Hospital, my parents had been staying with my dad's sister in the city. She gave me a Bible storybook and Mom would read to me often out of that book during my hospital stay. My dad's father was living with us and had never accepted Christ as his Lord and Savior. Mom had prayed for his salvation for many years. At the age of 87, he began to read my Bible storybook. Mom said that he would ask her about the pictures in the book. He wanted to know if the stories were true. Mom witnessed to him and finally one day he asked Mom if he could go to church with us. He was 88 years old when he gave his heart to the Lord.

My sister Janice told Walter that he had made a statement to her that if God was real; He would have to perform a miracle before his eyes before he would believe in Him. She said, "Walter, you were there the day Sherry was hit by the car and she is alive, walking, talking and gaining strength every day. I told you that God might prove His love to you by performing a miracle before your eyes. Sherry was that miracle. Now do you believe that God is real?" Walter responded to her, "I saw it with my very eyes. She should not be alive. God must be real to heal her body. He truly is a miracle-working God."

My mom was a prayer warrior. She made me believe in the power of prayer.

Mom went home to be with the Lord in December 2007, but I'm alive today because of her faith in God. She shared this story with me over and over as I was growing up and told me how I was a walking, talking miracle. My dad gave his heart to the Lord and is serving God today and still sharing this testimony with others. I have a husband, two sons and daughters-in law, and a daughter. All my children are honor students. I have a job and I am currently getting an associate's degree. In the spring of 2014, I was inducted into Phi Theta Kappa Honor Society at Eastern Oklahoma State College. God has truly done not just one, but many miracles in my life. I should not be able to function at all today or have any of the blessings God has bestowed on me. Because of prayer and God's miracle-working power, my cup runs over with God's blessings. I have overcome many obstacles in life and I can say that I am truly a product of the miracle-working power of God.

My Miracle Journey Back to Healthiness

By: Jane Huffman

"This is my story, this is my song!"

Without my knowledge, my journey had begun approximately 15 years prior to my climactic revelation in 2009. I realize one should never ask, "Why me, Lord?" Nevertheless, we are all only human and I believe it is a natural question when faced with a trial in life. December 11, 2009 is the date that will forever resonate in my mind. Isaiah 43:2 says, "When we go through deep waters and great trouble, I will be with you."

On Wednesday before Thanksgiving, I drove myself to our cabin located about an hour and a half from our house. I went ahead of Gary as he had to work, and he was to come up later that evening. To reach my destination, I had to take numerous twists and turns on unmarked roads through Weyerhaeuser clear-cuts, which are challenging to say the least. I wanted to get a head start on Thanksgiving dinner preparations for our yearly family get together. In retrospect, I will never truly understand how I safely arrived at the cabin without getting lost except by God's grace and His hand leading me. "Do not be afraid, for I am with you." Isaiah 43:5.

Thanksgiving day arrived and so did all the family; however, I had mentally checked out! The whole family enjoyed fellowship and the noon meal, but later in the day I could not remember the day's events or even my precious grandchildren having been there! My loving sister Nancy, who knows me so well, took my family aside and told them something was very wrong with me. Gary had previous knowledge of my falling, walking into door facings, and rolling out of bed, which were all very disturbing occurrences to him, so all of this was discussed thoroughly. My children, too, had begun noticing subtle differences in their mother. I was not the same Mama Jane I had always been. The group decision was unanimous; my problems had to be addressed.

The following day my son Sean privately called Nancy and asked that she take me to Dr. George Freeman, our primary care physician, for an examination. With the permission of the rest of the family, Nancy did just that. Dr. Freemans's examination was very thorough, and he concluded my visit with a CT scan at the hospital. With great anxiety we all awaited the outcome of the scan.

As I was driving home from town the next day, Dr. Freeman called me on my cell phone. Knowing I was driving, he told me to go home and he would give me a call back. With my persistence, he reluctantly gave me my CT results. I had a brain tumor about the size of a baseball in the frontal lobe of my brain.

As if in slow motion, I vaguely remember calling Gary, who was working on our ranch in Eagletown, and telling him, "I have a brain tumor." In my mind this was so unreal; no one in my family had ever had a brain tumor. This was something I had only read about or had known of others having. I know Gary was as traumatized as I, and neither of us knew which way to turn. Jesus said, "Do not let your hearts be troubled; trust in God and trust in me." John 14:1. My wise husband has always said, "When we find ourselves in a corner, there is only one place to turn in our hour of need and that is to God." Oh, the power of prayer! Thus, that is just what I did. I fervently prayed for a miraculous healing; I wasn't through living yet.

I truly believe there is a reason for everything, even if one may not understand what that reason is; but most probably it is to bring us to our knees and humble us before the Lord. I know that is what happened in our family. We all tend to take precious life for granted and forget we are never promised tomorrow.

What would we do without faith, love, and family? As confused as Gary and I both were, little did we know that the prayer wheels of our entire loving family were already in motion. They were and still are a "God send" in our lives. Not knowing how desperate or how dangerous my situation was, Dr. Freeman had the family moving as quickly as possible on my behalf. Our daughter Donna, who lives in Tulsa, was frantically trying to get referrals and locate the best neurosurgeon possible; my sister and brother-in-law were in charge of Gary and his travel arrangements; and last, but not least, my beautiful niece, Carla had volunteered to drive me to the emergency room, picking up Sean at his law office in Antlers on the way through. Looking back, I wonder how any of us functioned that day. Again, God was in charge.

I remember telling Carla that she was going to get a speeding ticket. Suddenly the lights began flashing and we were pulled over. The officer asked us what our hurry was and "Miss Take Charge Carla" just shook my CT scans in his face and said, "My aunt has a brain tumor and we're on our way to the ER in Tulsa." He quickly allowed us to continue on without a ticket.

As I was taken into the ER, again I realized God was in control and works in mysterious ways. Dr. David Fell, the physician on call, was the one and only neurologist who had been recommended to Donna. He assessed me that night and told the family who had all gathered by then that the findings were conclusive; and that surgery was needed as quickly as possible; however his schedule was so full I would have to wait another week with proper medications to get me through. That was the longest week of my life. The following day, Dr. Fell ran more tests and assured the family the tumor, known as a meningioma, would most probably be benign. He informed us that due to the size of the tumor, it must have been growing slowly for 15 years. He went on to say it was the largest of this type he had ever seen. All of the symptoms I had been experiencing were due to the vast amount of pressure on the front of my brain.

During this week of waiting, God gave me one of his greatest earthly angels to help get me through--my precious daughter. I stayed at her house until surgery could be performed the next Monday. She medicated me on schedule; she had to watch her mother go through the various stages of progression the doctor had informed her of and she had to deal with each one, all while caring for her own family's needs. Before one particular doctor's appointment, I remember sitting at Donna's vanity mirror and crying because I could not remember how to put my makeup on! She lovingly hugged me and said, "Mom, I've got this!" What would we do without our God-given children and the blessings they assure to us?

December 11, 2009, finally came, and I was admitted to St. Francis Hospital. We all prayed for the Lord's hand to be upon the skilled surgeon and me; a slip of the scalpel, too much or too little, would have damaging effects on me forever! Brother Laroi and Sister Jean Woods stood alongside all the family for "blessed assurance." I had enlisted another prayer warrior at home, my dear friend Erma Lee Griffin. If anyone had a direct connection to the Lord, it had to be this woman. Carol and her husband Jeff and Gary's sister Gail and her daughters also gathered with the rest of the family for prayer and support. As I was wheeled away that fateful day, I had such a calm and peace come over me. I knew I was in God's hands and He was not finished with me yet.

Six hours and four pints of blood later, Dr. Fell emerged from surgery with the good news to the family that he felt he had gotten the entire tumor, and it was most assuredly benign. I was moved to the Neuro ICU and remained there almost two weeks. During this time, Gary, Donna, and Nancy rotated turns staying with me. "I will lie down and sleep in peace, for you alone, O Lord, make me dwell in safety." Psalm 4:8. Now I definitely had a new hairdo and a metal plate on the front of my head, but all was good. "You restored me to health and let me live." Isaiah 31:16. I was a sight; thank the Lord for hair growing back!

Dr. Fell had been medically trained in the military, and his manner had always been all business until I was finally released. That momentous day he laughingly told me I had been very "bland" when he had initially met me, and it was good to see that I actually had a personality and could speak for myself. His next words were, "Well, I'm on to sick people!" We could all finally laugh. I thank the Lord daily that He put this surgeon in charge of my life. This was not just by chance but through divine providence. Dr. Fell loves Chilean wine, and Gary and I faithfully send him a Christmas gift basket of his favorites yearly in continued gratitude for him having saved my life. He was my Godsend.

After being released from the hospital, I had to remain in Tulsa at Donna's home until February in case of complications and for continued doctor checkups.

I received physical therapy to improve my motor skills, and home health care nurses came by daily for cleansing and bandaging my incision, which ran from one ear around to the other. Dr. Brollier, as I jokingly called him, my son-in-law, was rarely pleased with the job home health care performed. Every evening when he came in from work, he would examine their work, and if he wasn't pleased he would redo my bandages. He would say, "Mama Jane, trust me. I'm good with dogs." What a consolation! A little humor never hurts anyone.

My smallest grandchildren, at the time, were ages two and one. They didn't know what to think of their Mama Jane as they watched my progression through a spectrum of colors; first black, to purple, to green, to yellow, and finally to normality. Corey, my oldest grandchild, was often one of the brightest lights in my day. He would come in after a long day at school, and we would just sit around in the evenings talking and spending quality time together. A defining moment in my healing finally came, when for the first time, I felt like getting in the floor and playing Hot Wheels with Tristan, who was two. I knew I had finally come full circle at last! Unknown to me, Donna captured this picture, and I cherish it to this day.

During this extended stay at Donna's, both Gary and Sean had to work, but faithfully traveled to Tulsa and visited every weekend. Donna was designated "taxi" driver for my weekly checkups. As an added bonus for her, many of her friends pitched in with meals, babysitting, etc., during this time to relieve some of her pressure; I am sure she was feeling spread pretty thin between caring for me and caring for her own family. I never in all that time heard her utter a complaint; she just unconditionally loved and cared for me.

Beautiful flowers, numerous cards, letters, and phone calls flowed in from my wonderful Broken Bow family and beyond. I even heard from many of my former students during this convalescing time. I remained indefinitely on many church prayer lists, and I knew in my heart that the Lord heard these prayers for my continued healing. All this is to say, mine was a very humbling experience and made me so much more aware and responsive to others' troubles and needs.

The last week in February, Gary finally came to take me back to Broken Bow. Home had never looked so good. Again, friends and family surrounded us through visits, meals, cards, flowers, and prayers for my continued well-being.

Everyone knew, as we did, that there would always be a chance of recurrence. I continued for four years to receive CT scans and regularly scheduled neurological visits. When I arrived back home, a friend of mine said, "Jane, you were so lucky!" My response was, "Luck had nothing to do it; I was blessed." It was the Lord working His miracles. "I have shown you many great miracles from the Father." John 10:3. I will end this testimony of my journey to healthiness by citing part of one of my favorite church hymns, which resonates each time I hear it. "He touched me and made me whole." At this time, I am five and a half years out and healthy. THANK YOU LORD.

Repairing My Broken Heart

By: Jan Lee

When I was asked to give a testimony of God's work in my life, I went back to the year of 1998. Several events occurred that sent me into a deep depression for nine long months. My dad had died, the church we attended split, and we had some family difficulties. I shared with a pastor how my heart had been ripped out. Later that week, we went to a community revival. The preacher's sermon was titled, "Living In a Cave." After going to the altar, a lady came to me and shared her vision of a man in the line of duty who had his heart ripped out, and how Jesus had replaced it with a new heart.

The next day, I decided to leave my bedroom after months of depression and work on my yard fence. About 10 a.m., I went into the house for a drink of water. The phone rang. It was my dear mom, who had lain in bed the night before, singing the praise chorus "I See The Lamb." Mom told me Jesus had appeared to her. He was sitting, and as she looked down, I was sitting on His left leg and a wicker basket was on His right leg. As she looked at me, she noticed a gaping hole in my chest. Christ put a new heart in! Then, He put in little capsules, which came out of the basket. The capsules had words on them: Love, Joy, Peace, and other fruits of the Spirit. Mom called them Gospills (a play on the word "gospel").

Jesus started sewing my heart up, but then said, "I lack one more thing." He took something else out of the basket, but it would not go in because my heart had been sewn up so tightly. After several tries, He showed my mother the lettering on the capsule. The word was "forgiveness." I would have to forgive those who hurt me. The vision then faded out.

God knew I needed that confirmation from my dear mom. From that point, I started getting better. It took Christ to get me out of deep depression. Today, I am so thankful to Jesus for His work in placing the fruits of the Spirit in me and repairing my broken heart.

Anna Grace

By: Steve Lester

After a long, difficult labor and delivery our first child was born—a wonderful girl. After a brief hug by Tama, her mother, and a quick slurp of the nasal passages, a seasoned nurse whisked the baby away instructing me to follow. I was told to hold the baby as nurses made ready for weighing and measuring the child, etc. I kissed her and remember having a tingle down my spine in surprise at how soft a forehead can be. The nurses measured her length (22 inches I think), and then laid her on the scale. Eight pounds, two ounces. The date was the 8th day of the second month, 1992.

The baby was handed back to me. I was to follow the three nurses. While passing through a short hallway of sorts I noticed that the baby had stopped breathing. As composed as possible I told the head nurse. "Sometimes this happens," she said calmly. I handed the pale baby to her. The younger nurses became concerned. "Should we call someone?" one asked. "No. It will be alright," the older nurse said. The baby was lifeless, not breathing, beginning to turn blue. At least one minute had passed. The confident nurse began to blow gently into the baby's face, talking calmly to her. "Come on little girl. You have to breathe now." As time went on, the baby's color turned more and more blue. There was no response whatsoever. By now the two younger nurses were becoming somewhat frantic. "What do we do? What do we do?" The experienced nurse seemed less and less confident, doubling her efforts with increasing urgency.

I stood helpless—frozen with uncertainty and fear. I knew what was going on. I knew this was not routine. The thief and destroyer was trying to take my newborn baby as I stood by impotent and weak. Years of spiritual apathy had turned me into a 90-pound spiritual weakling. I realized that a godly father with strong faith would have courage to fight for his daughter. All I could do was stand and pray, "God please. God please. God please."

If this baby didn't breathe very soon there would never be an Anna Grace Lester. If she didn't take a breath right away we would lose our first child after all the anticipation and preparation. If this tiny thing did not get oxygen to her brain in a matter of seconds she would never say a prayer. She would never give me a hug. If this child did not respond right away she would never play April fools, love puppies or go to deer camp. She would never win a spelling bee, read the most books, or tell a stupid knock-knock joke. Many things hinged on whether or not this child took a breath in the next seconds. She would never write an award-winning story, sing a beautiful song, be valedictorian, or lead worship in her youth group. She would never go on mission trips. She would never win a teen pageant in a $10 dress. She would never be a Coca-Cola scholar or go to a private Christian University on faith and academic scholarships. She would never meet a godly man named Dustin or become the internal communications coordinator at the Assemblies of God headquarters in Springfield, MO. This baby needed to breathe immediately and all I could do was stand there and repeat, "Please God, please God."

After what may have been about three full minutes she finally took a breath. Her color returned and everything returned to normal. I remember the older nurse taking on a smug look that said, "I was never worried." I remember carrying her the rest of the way to the nursery with a heavy feeling of responsibility for the spiritual safety of this child. I sensed God's conviction. "You'd better man up, boy." We named her Anna Grace. Anna was chosen somewhat randomly and Grace was a cherished family name on Tama's side of the family. We were both 28 years old and we had our first child. Oh, my. The very next day both mother and baby were checked out of the hospital, wheeled out to the curb for the ride home. With the newborn in her car seat and Tama beside me I remember thinking, "What now? This isn't right. We should have to attend a seminar or something. What are we supposed to do? We don't know anything about babies." It was quite sobering.

Complications in delivery had left Anna with upper respiratory issues. She arrived home feeling poorly. She cried a lot. She struggled with nursing. She seemed generally miserable most all the time. We had our work cut out for us. Little did we know.

A couple of days after arriving home Tama got a call from a pediatric nurse. "We need you to bring the baby back for more blood testing. Something is irregular. PKU or something. Anyway, bring her back down here. Bye." Tama called me at school. This was pre-internet so I consulted my Mayo Clinic book of medical terminology. PKU—Phenylketonuria. A congenital disease with symptoms including mental retardation, behavioral and social problems, seizures, hyperactivity, stunted growth, albinism and more. The doctor trips began.

More blood tests were done. She did not have PKU. The nurse had been confused. (Nurses, if you don't know what you are talking about, don't say anything.) The tests showed that Anna was born with severe hypothyroidism. What little thyroid tissue Anna had was in the back of her tongue rather than down in her neck as normal. The thyroid regulates growth and brain development among other things, so without treatment Anna's diagnosis was dwarfism, mental retardation, and short life span. We were told that just 30 years prior this would not have been detected until it was too late as the test for this was not routine for newborns at that time. We were thankful that it had been caught right away. We had to crush a little pink pill once each day and give it to her dissolved in some liquid that she would take by bottle. No big deal really. In addition, we were taking Anna to Texarkana, about a one and a half hour drive, frequently for monitoring and regular blood tests. All the hormone therapy, etc. kept Anna irritable and cranky. Bless her heart... she just seemed miserable.

Anna had come home from the hospital with some bluish red streaks near her left eye, mouth, and back of the head. She also had a purple swelling under her tongue. We assumed these were caused from bruising in delivery. But they did not go away. They started to swell and look irritated. The pediatrician diagnosed them as hemangiomas—places of excess capillary concentration just under the skin. This was not serious, he told us. With time they will increase in size and darken in color. Since they are on the face she will probably want to undergo a new laser therapy when she's older to reduce discoloration. Don't worry about it for now. No big deal. So we didn't worry about it, even when the swelling shut her left eye. Anna was now about three months old.

On one of our many trips to the doctor, he became immediately concerned upon entering the room. "This baby's eye is swollen almost completely shut! Why have you not brought her down long before now?" 'Long before now' would have just been a few days sooner as we had probably been down there only a couple weeks before. "You told us not to worry about the hemangiomas," I replied. Once again the doctor ignored me because I was 'just the father.' (I kid you not) "We have to get this baby to a specialist right away. This is serious!" the doctor insisted. He made us an appointment in Little Rock Children's Hospital with a world-renown pediatric dermatologist, Dr. Kincannon. We felt like the young, ignorant parents that we were just following the health care carrot.

So off to Little Rock we went. Walking in that hospital will make one thankful for their blessings. We saw children with every possible affliction. It was heart breaking. We spent the night at a Ronald McDonald house and met parents who had never gotten to hold their eight-month-old child due to severe health complications. Suddenly Anna's problems seemed quite mild.

We took her in for the appointment. It was just a regular day. We were just doing what we knew to do. Life was somewhat crazy, but good. We got checked in and spent a short time in a waiting room. I read an article in a pediatric magazine about babies' brain development. We were taken back to a consultation room where we waited longer. Soon, Dr. Kincannon came in. He was younger than I had expected—probably mid 30's. He was cordial, but immediately serious upon picking up the baby. He probably had not been in the room a full minute when he said, "I will be back. DO NOT GO ANYWHERE. I will be back. It might take just a little bit, but I will be back. DO NOT GO ANYWHERE, STAY RIGHT HERE. PROMISE ME YOU WILL STAY RIGHT HERE." I heard him tell the nurse to stay right by the door and make sure we did not leave. Tama and I just looked at each other and shrugged. We weren't going anywhere.

After maybe 20 minutes the door opened and people of all ages, colors, shapes and sizes started filing into that little room. Dr. Kincannon introduced Dr. Waynor, pediatric dermatologist, Dr. Brodsky, pediatric ophthalmologist, and at least a dozen interns, nurses, and others. Suddenly I was wide-awake. The doctors took our baby and passed her around like it was "show and tell".

They poked, prodded, hummed and hawed. They seemed to communicate with each other with facial expressions and grunts, which were obviously over the heads of us simpletons. Interns were furiously taking notes, very somber and studious. After several minutes Dr. Kincannon said, "We will be back soon. DO NOT GO ANYWHERE. We will be back. YOU STAY RIGHT HERE." He made us promise again. The nurse was stationed on guard again. We weren't shrugging anymore.

Dr. Kincannon came back with fewer people this time. Tama was holding the baby. The doctor sat down in an office chair. He scooted right up in our personal space and put a hand on each of our knees. He paused and looked us in the eye. He took a breath and said, "We are pretty sure that we can save her eyesight." What??? "We're pretty sure we can save her eyesight," he repeated. "You see, the hemangioma has invaded her eye socket, crowding her eyeball, interrupting function on that side. She likely has headaches. In addition, her left eyelid is swollen shut to the point that her little brain is now ignoring vision from that eye. At this stage of development, this will cause that eye to go blind. And at this crucial stage, if one eye goes blind, the other will probably lose its sight as well." The thief had tried to take my little girl's life. He had tried to render her mentally incapacitated, and now he was trying to steal her vision.

The plan was laid out. Anna would have to wear a patch over her good eye that would force the brain to acknowledge vision from the swollen side. She would be put on an aggressive steroid treatment of prednisone to reduce swelling enough to perform a surgery. The surgery would entail implanting crystals into the eye socket in order to shrink hemangioma swelling there. All this was to take place over the next several weeks. We would make many trips to Little Rock. Meanwhile, she needed to be fitted for eyeglasses.

Really??? Glasses on a three-month-old baby? How's this going to work? I was very skeptical, but if you've ever been on the health care roller coaster you know what I'm saying… you just do what they tell you and don't ask questions.

Dr. Brodsky explained that for a baby it is not important that their vision is clear— just the same on each side. That way the brain will attend equally to the signals coming in from both eyes and development will be normal. "How in the world do you determine the prescription?" was my question. He didn't answer, just demonstrated. Anna was strapped into a very tight papoose-like straight jacket. Only her little face was not bound up with straps and laces. She was not happy about that and tried to let us know, but even her chubby little cheeks were held tightly enough to limit her fussing. Dr. Brodsky stood over her with a light strapped to his forehead, a prism, ruler, and magnifying glass in his hands. He shone the light through the prism, creating a rainbow on the back of her retina. With the ruler he measured the width of color bands created inside Anna's little eyes. He explained that he had to determine the eyeglass prescription that would result in identical rainbows for each eye. With hands full, he began to perform difficult mathematical calculations in his head as he muttered aloud. I recognized math terms I had heard, but did not understand. Sines and cosines and tangents and derivatives. Either that man was quite a genius or he sure knows how to run a good bluff. One way or another, he pretty soon stood up straight, laid down his tools, took out a simple little pad and wrote down some scribbles that I could not make heads nor tails of. "Here, take this to the eyeglass store down the street and they'll fix you up."

Anna was fitted with little pink glasses that had an elastic strap around the back. Surprisingly she never tried to take them off or mess with them. From the very start she wore them happily. She was quite a sight. After a couple weeks on the prednisone she was swollen up like a mad little horny toad. Her eye was still mostly swollen shut and the pink glasses just set it all off nicely.

We took her home in anticipation of the surgery. She had to wear the patch for a certain length of time each day, the glasses the rest of the time. We had to give her steroids daily as well as her daily thyroid pill. She still didn't feel well and would not sleep at night.

Even at this early age she loved books. Tama and I took turns rocking her and reading at night. Many nights she would not sleep until the wee hours of morning. Tama and I would take turns soothing her. She loved for us to sing also. Rock, read, sing. Rock, read, sing. Switch parents. Rock, read, sing. Rock, read, sing.

Tama had quit her accounting job to care for the baby. I taught school, drove a route bus, and coached basketball. We were exhausted. There were many times Tama would call her mother to come over and care for the baby so she could get a nap. My mother lived a few hours away at the time, but was able to help out on several occasions. During that time I developed a strong compassion for young, single mothers who are abandoned to care for small children all alone. Tama and I were 29 years old by now, both with stable family support systems, steady income, and college degrees. Most of all we had each other for support. And yet there were nights when each of us thought we just couldn't do it anymore. The baby would cry and often there was just no comforting her. I often wondered how a young single parent with no support could possibly cope.

Meanwhile, Tama and I were both sobering up spiritually. We had resumed faithful church attendance and begun to pray together. I had grown up in a very strong Christian home and God's Word had been taught to me from day one. I knew that God had appointed me as spiritual leader of my home and that I was responsible in that regard. I also knew that my family would either enjoy blessing or lack based upon my spiritual leadership. I began to pray, "God, prepare my heart to be totally committed to you." God was bringing us in line with His will.

One Sunday Morning, Pastor LaRoi Woods told Tama and me to go to the nursery and get Anna. We brought her to the front of the auditorium. He read the scripture from James, chapter 5, "Is anyone among you sick? Let him call for the church, and let them pray over him, anointing him with oil in the name of the Lord. And the prayer of faith will save the one who is sick, and the Lord will raise him up." Many church elders came forward and prayed over our baby, anointing her with oil in obedience to God's Word. Sometimes we don't understand why God instructs as he does. Probably the blind man who got mud smeared in his eyes thought that was a little strange. But the simple principle is that God honors obedience. Many times when I deal with a spiritual issue, my emotions may not be stirred. God doesn't respond to emotion. He is moved by obedience to His Word. When we obey, God is faithful. That morning as those wonderful people prayed over my daughter I knew that the fervent prayer of righteous people accomplishes much. I knew that my baby was in God's hands.

One evening Anna was able to sleep in her crib and Tama had gone to bed. It was only a few days before the scheduled surgery. I was in the living room praying and reading the Bible. My parents had given me a book by T.L. Osborn entitled *Healing the Sick*. I started reading that book. T.L. and Daisy Osborn had been missionaries in about every part of the world and had witnessed many thousands of documented miracles. The book describes account after account of simple people believing the simple message that God's Word really means what it says. As I read that book I knew that it was true and my faith began to grow. The simple message from God's Word was perfectly clear as I read through the night. "He sent His Word and healed them, and delivered them from all their infirmities. Jesus went about doing good and healing all that were oppressed of the devil, for God was with Him." "He was wounded for our transgressions... and by His stripes we were healed." "God is no respecter of persons. Jesus said, 'I am willing. Be made whole.' " On and on my faith was increased as I read the accounts in the book, then looked up the scriptures about physical healing in my Bible. The hours passed long into the early morning. I needed sleep badly, but my spirit was being fed Truth and strength. There was an instant in time when I came to the realization, "God is in control. Everything is going to be alright." I believe God granted me a gift of faith at that moment. Suddenly I was at absolute perfect peace. I was not worried. I was not troubled in any way. I had complete confidence in God's faithfulness and his Sovereignty; I had no preconceived notions about how everything was going to unfold. I did not hear a voice. I did not see an angel. I did not get goose bumps. My emotions were in complete neutral. But in my spirit I knew beyond a doubt that God was going to take care of my girl and take care of my wife and me. I went in to where Anna was sleeping. I laid my hand gently on her back and prayed just like this... "God, your word is true. Jesus paid the price for Anna's healing on the cross. I am a believer. I am laying my hand on her according to your Word. I ask you to heal her in the name of Jesus. Thank you." I walked into my bedroom and went to sleep with perfect peace.

The day of the surgery came. We stayed once again at the Ronald McDonald house at no charge. Anna had to report for surgery at 5:30 a.m. The nurses put her in a little gown. They gave her a little pill and put her in a special baby bed with wheels. She could not eat or drink so she had an empty bottle to suck on. Dr. Brodsky came out and told us very briefly about the procedure. He said that it would not take long. So just like that, a team of strangers wheeled our baby girl away through a pair of big swinging doors. She was mad and crying. So was her mother.

Tama and I prayed together once again, and then settled in for the duration. In no time at all Dr. Brodsky came back through the double doors with a bewildered expression on his face. He came over and sat on a coffee table in front of us. (Dr. Brodsky is brilliant, but very direct.) "Your daughter does not need surgery." What? "I'm not sure why, but the hemangioma in her eye socket is gone. We will not need to inject the crystals. She can go home. Everything is OK. I am very surprised." I said, "Doctor, God healed my daughter and I am not surprised." He just said, "OK." Then he left. I suspect that in his career he has witnessed many of these surprises.

This is the part of the story where you think I will say Tama and I shouted praise the Lord, assembled all the people in the waiting room, and led fourteen souls to Christ. Nope. We just sat there looking at each other like the ignorant young parents we really were, knowing that God had healed our girl. Soon enough the nurses brought our baby out and we went home.

A couple days after the non-surgery, Anna started pulling at her glasses. We would spat her hand and say, "NO. Leave your glasses on." We wrestled with her for several days until we took her to Dr. Brodsky for a checkup. We told him about her recent habit of taking her glasses off. He examined her and said, "She is taking her glasses off because they are obstructing her vision. Her eyes are normal. She does not need glasses anymore." I said, "Dr. Brodsky, God healed my daughter." He said, "OK." Then he left.

At infancy, doctors had warned us that Anna's hemangiomas would grow, spread, and darken into unsightly port wine stains. We were told that this would trouble her in her junior high years as she became increasingly aware of her appearance. She would probably opt to undergo somewhat painful procedures to minimize the markings. This would all be very expensive. Insurance probably would not pay since it was cosmetic. Gloom, despair, and agony on me... on and on... So on and so forth. Well I am here to report... the very opposite of all that happened. The hemangiomas shrunk to almost gone. If you met my gorgeous newlywed daughter today you would not even see the tiny little red streak over her left eye, nor the natural lip liner that remains. Under her tongue is perfectly fine. I don't know and don't care what happened to the spot in the back of her head because it's covered with beautiful brown hair. This was all true long before Jr. High School and she adjusted very well through those years, thank you very much. She did have to wear glasses for a short while in late elementary school and her eyes aren't perfect to this day, but that has nothing to do with aggressive capillary growth. And guess what… She is alive. She is brilliant. She has good vision. Her entire life has been a continuous string of miracles of every sort. And guess what else… God healed her of hypothyroidism in the meantime! I was told I could only tell one story for now. Maybe I'll get to tell that one another time.

When Anna was four, our second daughter was on the way. While looking for baby names we learned the meaning of the name Anna. It is "GRACE." So our eldest child is essentially named Grace Grace. And indeed she enjoys God's double portion.

The Gordon Manning Story

By: Gordon and Ginger Manning

The last thing Gordon Manning remembers about Jan. 2, 2001 was seeing the lights of a vehicle coming down the road behind him. He doesn't remember the impact or anything that happened in the tragic accident, which almost took his life and ultimately ended his career as a trooper with the Oklahoma Highway Patrol.

The day of his accident began as a typical day for Gordon, trying to help out where he was needed. A big ice storm had hit Oklahoma only days before and covered almost the entire county with ice. There were power outages everywhere and many roads were closed.

Gordon's regular job was primarily in lake patrol, but for him the "bottom line" was to do what needed to be done. During the summer months his responsibilities, as part of a six-man dive team, took him from one county to another recovering bodies, vehicles and anything else to do with water. "We were good at what we did," Gordon said. "And we were often called to assist in other states because we had more training than teams in many of the states."

With little traffic on the lakes in the winter, Gordon had been working on an assignment to do background checks on applicants for the next highway patrol academy. Tuesday was his regularly scheduled day off, but he was trying to finish in-home interviews with the applicants and decided to go ahead and work. Gordon called to set up an interview, but the applicant's mother said they needed to put it off because a tree had fallen during the ice storm and was lying in her front room.

He called headquarters at Durant reporting the cancellation of his interview and could have taken his day off. However, there were people in his own community who had been without water for three days. Gordon went right to work rounding up chainsaws and some men from the local volunteer fire department to help. They worked all morning cutting downed trees trying to get roads cleared north of Valliant.

"I remember Peggy's Cafe was the only place in town open so I stopped there to eat lunch," he recalled. "I had just walked out of the café when Kirby Byassee called me. He was the only trooper working and he asked if I would come help him with a truck accident south of Idabel. I said sure. It was close to Waterfall Creek on SH 259. I parked my patrol unit off the road and left my emergency lights on. I walked about a quarter of a mile down the road to check out the water level and damage from the ice storm. I could see about a mile down the road. As I began to make my way back, I turned to see a pickup truck coming toward me, but he was on his side of the road. The last time I looked, he was probably 60 yards behind me. The next thing I remember is waking up 20 days later, asking what happened."

Most of the information about the accident, Gordon learned from people at the scene and from the accident report: At approximately 6:18 p.m., an elderly man, driving a pickup truck struck Gordon from behind, knocking him 59 feet down the roadway. The accident report noted that a 30-foot trail of debris from Gordon's uniform was scattered on the road, and that fibers from a white sock on his right foot were found in the pavement. Officials said that the time of day might have been a factor in why the driver had not seen Gordon. He told Trooper Byassee that his cruise was set on 60 mph, and that he knew he had hit something, but didn't know what.

"I don't know how long I lay there," Gordon said. "But it was just before dark when I was hit. A Public Service dispatcher out of Tulsa came by and found me on the side of the road. He said he started talking to me to try to keep me conscious. He said I was bleeding badly and he knew I was about to go into shock. He pulled off his coat and put it over me. Because he was a dispatcher, he knew how to use a radio. I had three radios in my unit, and only the Good Lord could have shown him which radio to use, because the first one he reached for was the only one that would transmit in that area. Kirby heard him radio for help, stating, 'A trooper is down; he has been run over, he needs help.'

It's amazing how people make simple decisions without even noticing when they make them. Gordon had made a simple choice that day to wear his bullet-proof vest. "I seldom wore my vest, but for some reason I had put it on that day. Later, doctors told me there were three reasons why I survived the accident: First, I was in excellent physical condition; second, I had my vest on; and third, the Good Lord wasn't ready for me yet. I told the doctor he was right, but he had the reasons in the wrong order."

The pickup truck struck Gordon's left side below his gun belt line. His injuries included a broken pelvis, which was broken down the middle, along with both iliac wings being severely fractured. His pelvis proved to be his most painful and serious injury. His right leg was broken below his knee; his left lung was punctured, causing it to collapse; his cheek bones were broken; his upper palate was broken, torn loose and teeth were knocked out; his forehead was shattered; his nose was broken; his upper and lower sinuses were crushed and his cranium was fractured; his left arm sustained multiple injuries: the ligaments were torn loose from his shoulder and the joint was badly damaged; he also lost two inches of bone in his left arm, including the elbow joint.

At about 6:45 that evening, Gordon's wife, Ginger received a phone call that her husband had been in an accident. She wasn't sure just how serious it was until she saw his face. Later, Gordon learned that the EMTs had lost him twice in the ambulance during the 8-mile trip to the Idabel hospital. From Idabel, he was airlifted to Wadley Hospital in Texarkana.

Doctors told Ginger that Gordon's condition "didn't look good and the first 48 hours [were) the most critical." She was further told that if he did live, there was a possibility he would have brain damage and there was no absolute assurance he would ever walk again.

Despite what Doctors were saying, within a few days Ginger began to see miracles happening with Gordon.

"The day after his accident, the doctor came out and told me Gordon had a slow bleeder somewhere. 'We're going to have to go in and find it or he's going to bleed to death,' I was told." Already, he had been given 26 units of blood. The doctor said they would perform an angioplasty in the lower trunk area, first. If they could not locate it on the first attempt, they would have to try again going in through his shoulder and down through his heart. "I don't know anything about medical procedures," Ginger declared, "but, I knew that as much trauma as his body had taken, if they went through his heart, he might not survive." I thought, "Lord, his heart can't take much more." So, I went up to the ladies' room and locked the door. I got down on my knees and I got serious with God. I made promises to God that I intended to keep. About 20 minutes later I came out, believing and feeling that God had heard me. There were all these people waiting: our family, friends, and troopers who knew how to take control of the worst kinds of situations. Yet, it was like this was just happening to Gordon and me, and God was the only one who was in control and could help us. About 45 minutes into the procedure, the phone rang. I answered it. The voice said, 'Mrs. Manning, this is the radiologist.' My heart almost stopped. Then I heard him say, 'I'm just calling to tell you that we found the bleeder and it had already coagulated. We didn't even have to complete the procedure we had planned.' He continued, 'I don't know what happened, but your husband is doing fine.' I said to him, 'Let me tell you what happened. I've been on my knees for the last 20 minutes, asking for God's help. That's what happened. God stopped the bleeding.'"

During a two-week period, while Gordon was undergoing various surgeries, doctors would bring him out of a coma just long enough for Ginger to talk to him. She would tell Gordon what doctors had scheduled for him each day. "I didn't want him to be afraid," she said. "My greatest worry was that he would be afraid."

The accident happened on Tuesday and by Saturday, Gordon had already undergone several surgeries. Saturday morning was to be his biggest and longest surgery. It took the doctors more than 8 hours to reconstruct his pelvis. Up to this point, they had wrapped him with a wide band to help hold his pelvis together and keep him from bleeding profusely. Doctors would also reconstruct his facial bones and rebuild his sinus cavities. A neurologist would be present during surgery in case Gordon's fractured cranium required additional repair. This surgery would determine whether he had suffered any damage to his brain.

"When I went into ICU that morning, I told Gordon we were going to have to get in church when all this was over, He nodded his head. I asked him if he knew how to pray, and he nodded again, that made me feel a lot better," she acknowledged.

Thus far, Gordon had not been able to tell Ginger the one thing he actually remembered about his accident: In the blur of everything, Gordon remembered clearly, that at some point he had stood before God. And, he was certain, if God opened his book of life, he would split hell wide open. "1 can only tell you that I saw a massive book being laid atop a huge desk. It remained unopened, as an arm, dressed in a long, white sleeve, lay across it. I did all the things I swore I'd never do. I cried, my knees shook uncontrollably, and I begged, 'God, I don't want to go to hell; please don't let me go to hell.' I was screaming and crying, begging God to not send me to hell. You see I knew there was nothing I could do then to change that account. After God let me beg and cry and plead (those things that I always swore I'd never do, not even for my own life), in His great voice of mercy, God said, '1 can't make that choice for you. You have to make it yourself.' I said, 'God I'll do anything you ask, just please, don't let me go to hell.' He said, 'Son, I wasn't really ready for you right now. I've got some things I want you to do. If you'll do them, I'll let you.' And, just as quickly as I stood before Him, I was swept away, unable to recount the experience until some time later.

In the days that lay ahead, Gordon would come to know about *"walking through the valley of the shadow of death."* He would also understand plainly, that there was a God of mercy and most tender love who would lead him down that path. Pain would become his constant companion. For weeks, he would not know what it was like not to hurt all over his body. He fully believes that only the prayers of the people of God from many churches gave him back his life. He also knows without his wife, he could never have survived his most painful times. Ginger comes closest to knowing just how painful that path has been for Gordon. And he knows that her love and compassion gave her the strength to stay by his side for the 98 days he was in the hospital. "Ginger helped me in ways I can never say. She did things for me no one should ever have to do for another. Yet, she did them without hesitation," he smiled.

Thirty days after his accident, Gordon was moved from Wadley Hospital to a rehabilitation center in Texarkana. "We had been there for about four or five days, when a psychologist came in one morning to talk to Gordon," Ginger recalled. Gordon had made some remarks, not really saying that he had stood before God, but little things that put questions in the doctor's mind. He told Gordon that it was possible he might have some desperate feelings, implying that he might become suicidal. Gordon said, "Doc, I came too close to death. Why would I want to do anything to put myself back in that position again?'

"Gordon continued to say things that I couldn't understand. I was trying to prepare myself that he might have suffered some brain damage, after all. One night, he was in a tremendous amount of pain and we were both really down. I was sitting beside him, silently praying for God to touch him and ease his pain. That night was one of the darkest times for us. We both felt so very alone. He asked if I had my Bible. I told him that I did, and he asked me to read something to him. I didn't know what to read. I was just so lonely and sad and homesick. I began to pray, 'God, give me something from your Word that will bring us both comfort.' I opened my Bible and the first scripture I saw was Psalms 40, which says, *"I waited patiently for the Lord, and He inclined unto me and heard my cry. He brought me up also out of a horrible pit, out of the miry clay, and set my feet upon a rock, and established by goings. And He hath put a new song in my mouth, even praise unto our God.*" I could hardly read for the tears that were streaming down my face. The next line read: *"Many shall see it, and fear, and shall trust in the Lord.* " It was as though everything became clear that the reason we were in this predicament was for Gordon to be a living witness of God's power. I told Gordon I didn't understand what he had been referring to when he spoke of coming close to death, and if he didn't want to talk about it, I would understand. Gordon just pulled the sheet over his head and began crying, telling me about his experience with God. I'd never seen him react in such a way. I must say that I was afraid the injury to his head was becoming evident. I thought I'd better start preparing myself to cope with a Gordon I did not know. Later, I began to notice that when he would tell this story, he would give the same exact details every time. When it actually became real to me, and I knew it wasn't hallucinations or caused by the lick to his head, was when he said, 'I was standing in this line and my knees were shaking. I was scared to death. I knew I was standing before God.' He said he looked behind him and couldn't see the end of the line. What made me know he was talking with a clear mind, was when he said, I looked behind me and I thought, 'Manning, this is not good.' I've heard him say that so many times about different situations he's been in. I knew then, that what he experienced was real."

"There's so much to tell," Ginger continued. "But, one thing we know for certain is that his experience makes it clear why the accident happened and why Gordon is still alive: All God's purposes in Gordon's life have not been fulfilled."

Throughout his hospital stay including his time in rehab, Ginger kept a daily journal. She recorded all his surgeries, things he said, his notes, the first thing he ate when he came out of ICU, all the phone calls, people who visited and the many miracles that God performed for Gordon. Keeping the journal helped to occupy her mind and gave her something to do while she sat day and night at Gordon's bedside. Once, he questioned her about what happened. She told him and the next question was typical for Gordon, "did it tear up my unit?" Of course Ginger explained that his patrol unit was not involved in the accident. She noted that Gordon never lost his sense of humor. One day she asked him how he was feeling. His answer was, "I feel like I was drinking milk and the cow fell on me."

During his two-week stay at the rehabilitation center in Texarkana, Gordon had endured his most severe pain. Ginger had requested he be taken off morphine because he wasn't speaking or thinking rationally. "I knew Gordon wouldn't want to not be himself, if he could have thought clearly," said Ginger. "And I knew he'd rather endure some pain than depend on medication. Beginning the second week there, Gordon just couldn't take it anymore. Doctors were giving him all the oral pain medication they could at that time. Finally, he said, 'we are going to have to get a hold of God or you are going to have to take me back to Wadley and have them turn out my lights,'" Ginger recalled his desperation.

Gordon had a knot on his lower back that Ginger estimated to be the size of a small dinner plate, and a hematoma on his right hip about the size of a hot dog bun. "The pain was unbearable," she declared. Nurses had brought some analgesic cream for her to use, but she couldn't apply it because Gordon couldn't stand for her to touch the hematoma. "That night we prayed and prayed again," Ginger said. "I rubbed his forehead for about 45 minutes before he finally drifted off to sleep."

'"The next morning I looked into Gordon's eyes and I thought 'they look pretty clear, today.' I could look at his eyes in the morning and tell what kind of day he was going to have. I asked him how he felt. He said, 'pretty good. ' I remember pulling up the leg of his shorts, and I started to cry. I began saying, 'Thank you, God!' Gordon asked what was wrong and I told him, 'the hematoma is gone.' It was completely gone. That happened overnight. It just disappeared. I called for a nurse. I first asked her how long it would take for a hematoma the size of Gordon's to go away. She said it would most likely take several months. I pulled up his short's leg and said, 'Look, it's gone!' The nurse could hardly believe it. She exclaimed, 'I wouldn't have believed it if I hadn't seen it myself.' The knot on Gordon's back had also decreased to about the size of a small orange."

Ginger was determined that Gordon would walk again and that she would one day have her husband back good as new. She felt that Gordon was not getting the necessary therapy in Texarkana due to the extent of his injuries. For example, nothing was wrong with his right arm, yet nothing was being done to strengthen it. She went to Wal-Mart and bought some 2-pound dumbbells. Gordon would lie in bed and exercise his good arm in an effort to restore his strength.

At last, she called Gordon's liaisons and told them they had to get Gordon into Jim Thorpe Rehabilitation Center in Oklahoma City. She had been told Jim Thorpe was the best rehabilitation center that Oklahoma, Texas, or Arkansas had to offer. It was highly acclaimed for its success in injuries such as Gordon's and many Oklahoma State troopers have rehabilitated there. It was ultimately due to the extraordinary efforts of his superior officers including the Chief of the Oklahoma Highway that on Feb. 15, Gordon was transported to Jim Thorpe to begin his rehabilitation.

"An ambulance service was chartered to take me to Oklahoma City," Gordon said. "I still couldn't stand to be touched. They made a bed for me out of egg crate (foam rubber), and I was heavily medicated at the outset of the trip. Paramedics were authorized to give me morphine just in case I couldn't take the pain. An Oklahoma Highway Patrol car escorted us all the way.

"It was about a week before therapists began putting me in the heated pool. Being a diver, I knew if I could get in the pool I could move without it hurting so badly. Doctors hadn't told me that 1 might never walk again. They told Ginger, but not me." Gordon thought if he could keep getting in the pool that would be the turning point toward his recovery. He asked to be put in the pool twice each day instead of only once. Ginger made the request and it was approved.

"It was a major ordeal, just to get Gordon from the wheelchair back into bed," Ginger said. ''He couldn't put any weight on his legs and he had only one good arm with which to help lift himself," she explained. "I would get him on a slide board, and finally into bed. I would remove his swimsuit as quickly, but as gently as I could. I would throw blankets over him because he would be freezing by the time we got him from the first floor, where the pool was located, to our room on the second floor. Then I would use a hair dryer to warm and dry him under the covers. Usually, he would be asleep before I could finish the entire routine."

Gordon had lost 50 pounds in three weeks time. "The food at Jim Thorpe was great, Ginger said, "but Gordon couldn't chew anything." The injury to his upper palate made chewing almost impossible because his teeth (what were left) didn't align. Additionally, he could only partially open his mouth. "I went to Target and bought Ensure. I would make Gordon milkshakes using Ensure and ice cream, hoping to put some weight back on him."

"Once, I told Ginger I would kill for a hamburger, tater tots and a milkshake," Gordon grinned. She said, "but you can't chew it." I said, "You just go get me one, I'll figure out what to do with it. Ginger mashed the tater tots flat and gave me one small pinch at a time of the hamburger. It took almost an hour for me to eat it, but I ate every bite. It tasted so good," exclaimed Gordon.

"Kirby Byassee would come to the Oklahoma City sometimes on Tuesday and Thursday and he would come by and eat with us," Ginger recalled. "Gordon didn't particularly like the food that was served on those days, so I would go to Long John Silvers and get Gordon some soft fish. Kirby would take Gordon's tray and I got a tray each meal just like Gordon 's. It was good for Gordon to get to eat again with Kirby," she smiled. "Often, Gordon and I would trade out things off our trays. I would give him my bacon in exchange for his cold cereal (which he couldn't eat anyway). We had a system: I would feed Gordon a bite of food, and while he was trying to chew it, I could usually get in two bites for myself. I would give him a drink and I would take a drink. Little things you don't normally think about become so important in a situation like ours.

"At one point, Gordon began to develop a bed sore from lying in one position so long. I asked one of his nurses what we could do to stop it. She said to gently massage it and keep the blood circulating. It would hurt so badly that I would get up every 15 minutes or so day and night to massage it. I knew if I could do anything to keep him from developing a bed sore, I was going to because he had been through more than enough pain."

Ginger began doing most of Gordon's daily care, including bathing him, also changing his clothes and bed linens. "It was easier for Gordon to communicate to me what he wanted and when he hurt," she explained. "From watching the nurses, I learned how to wrap his arm. He had three different casts to use. He would tell the nurses when it was too tight and they would have to unwrap it. I wrapped it so many times that I got better at wrapping it than the nurses. I guess from Gordon being a machinist, he had to have everything exactly right, even to the 1000th of an inch. When I wrapped his arm, the end of the bandage had to come out at the same exact spot every time."

"The doctors kept me so doped up that for 78 days I had no bodily functions," Gordon said. "Everything just shut down because of all the codeine in my system. The nurses would perform the necessary routine procedures in order to keep my body functioning properly. Ginger was told she would have to learn to do them because it would be a way of life for me. I told them, 'No way, that wasn't going to happen.' I knew the effect pain medication had on one's body, and I knew I would have to get off the stuff if my body was ever going to function normally.

"I got serious with God about helping me get off the pain drugs. I decided if I were going to hurt, it would be for a reason and with a clear mind. I had been taking Oxycodone and Loritab every four hours around clock. I told Ginger I wasn't taking any more pain pills. She went to Wal-Mart and bought some Tylenol, which didn't help at all. She went back and bought some Ibuprofen.

"When my doctor came in one morning, she said they were increasing my pain medication. I said, 'I'm alright, Doc.' She said, 'I'm ordering the increase; you don't have to hurt.' I told her then that I had not had any pain medication for the past three days. She said, 'you can't do that.' I said, 'Sure I can, Doc. The only thing I have to do is die and pay taxes.' I said, 'I came real close to dying and I'm going to see what I can do about the taxes. And, I don't intend to take another pain pill.' She turned around and walked out. In a little while, she came back and said they were taking my medication off rotation, but if I needed it, I should call for it. I told her I wasn't hurting any worse than before. I could tell she was certain I would be calling for more pain medicine, but I never did.

"The next day one of the doctors came in and told me I would have to be on some kind of medication for the rest of my life to help with my bodily functions. He said I would have to go through an urodynamic test to see what kind of medication would be best for me. I couldn't sit in my wheelchair with a three-inch thick air cushion and a two inch-thick egg crate for more than five minutes. The urodynamic test was going to take one and one-half hours on a hard-bottom chair. I knew I couldn't stand the pain. The doctor repeated what nurses had told Ginger-that certain procedures and the medications would become a way of life for me. I told him it would not become a way for life for me, because God was going to heal me. 'Okay,' the doctor said, 'God has until Friday; otherwise, you're taking the test.' This was on Wednesday. Ginger and I knew that, once again, we must call on God for a miracle. We began praying earnestly. That afternoon, Ginger took me to the pool for my therapy. Not long after we got back to my room, God answered one of our prayers. By morning, God had completely restored my bodily functions.

When the doctor came in on Friday morning, he said, 'I hear you got out of taking the tests.' I said, 'Yeah, Doc, is this a miracle or what?' He didn't say anything. I asked again, 'Doc, is this a miracle?' He just grunted, 'yeah,' then turned around and walked out. That was the last time I saw him.

"From that time until now, I still haven't taken any pain pills. All I take now is one Aleve in the morning. Sure, I hurt and I'm sore all the time, but at least I'm in control of my body and mind.

"We had three or four nurses who came in our room every night and prayed with us," Gordon said. "One night one of the nurses came in and said they were not allowed to pray with us anymore. Boy, Ginger walked out to find a supervisor. She said, 'listen, as long as we're here what we do in our room is our business.' The nurse explained that some people would sue if a nurse prayed in their room. This is sad, but true," Gordon said.

Gordon and Ginger know, without a doubt, Gordon would not have survived the accident in the first place, except for the miracle-working power of God. Still, the voice that thundered in his brain, "If you're tough, you can do this," kept him fighting. And the love for her husband that knew no bounds gave Ginger an extraordinary capacity for sacrifice. At night she would massage Gordon's feet and legs, then lift and bend them just like the therapists did during the day.

"On March 27, I watched with tears of joy and thankfulness, as Gordon summoned all his strength and courage-and with tears in his eyes too-he took his first steps since January 2. Chief Gary Adams, of the Oklahoma Highway Patrol also witnessed Gordon's 30 steps that day. It was a milestone for us-one that we'll never forget or take lightly, " Ginger avowed.

The following day, March 28, Gordon and Ginger received the good news that they would be leaving Jim Thorpe within two weeks. The next stop would be home!

Meanwhile, prayer and Gordon's sheer determination was working. Gordon would be exhausted, but each day he would walk a little further. Gradually, he was gaining strength in his legs and lower body. However, he still had a decision to face about his missing elbow. Doctors had given him a ten percent chance for keeping his arm. We had petitioned Mayo Clinic for a cadaver elbow," Gordon recalls. "The answer was that it couldn't be done. We were told that because of my massive injuries, the anti-rejection drugs would cause more problems and that I probably wouldn't live three months. My only option for an elbow was an artificial one, and then I was made to understand there was a 90 percent chance I would lose my arm if an infection developed. I was told to go home and think about what I wanted to do about the elbow."

On April 10, ninety-nine days after his accident, Gordon was released from Jim Thorpe. The day before, Ginger made a flying trip home to clean her house and get things ready for his homecoming. "The last time I was home was Feb. 10. I came home from Texarkana to get some clothes and to tell Mama and my daughter, Emily 'goodbye,' before we moved Gordon to Oklahoma City. I didn't know how long it would be before I would see them again. I remember hugging them both. Pulling out from our driveway, I kept looking back at our home, wondering how long we would be away. I kept turning my head to look, trying to capture the image of home so it would stay fresh in my mind until our return. I could hardly see to drive for the tears," Ginger recalls.

Now, my flowers were blooming and my poppies were waist high in my flowerbeds. Everything looked so different, yet so familiar. I remember driving down Rufe road. When I got almost to the corner of the Slim Church of Christ, less than a mile from our house, I saw Neal Mussett and he waved at me. I started crying. I can't tell you how good it felt to have someone recognize me and speak to me because they knew me rather than just to be nice.

"The next morning, Emily drove me to Antlers to meet Gordon's partner and friend, Trooper Kevin Antwine. The Highway Patrol wanted Gordon to arrive home in a marked patrol unit and Gordon had requested that Kevin be the one to bring him home. Captain Gerald Davidson of the Oklahoma Highway Patrol insisted that he follow Gordon home. Captain Davidson did so much to help us; we can never thank him enough," Ginger stated. Gordon rode part of the way home with Kevin and part with Captain Davidson.

"When we arrived home, some of the family had put up a huge sign on the front of our house that read, 'Welcome Home, Gordon and Ginger!' Some of our friends were there, waiting for us to get home. It was nice," Ginger smiled.

Captain Davidson had asked me right after the accident, where I wanted Gordon's unit taken to. I told him that Kirby Byassee's house would be the safest place. My only request was that, when Gordon came home, his unit be parked in the driveway just as though he had driven it home himself. And, Kirby did just that. "

Ten days later, they returned to Jim Thorpe where Gordon would undergo surgery to replace his elbow. Doctors reminded him again that his chances were slim for saving his arm. "I told them I would take the ten percent chance; for them to do their job and let God do the rest" Today, Gordon's elbow doesn't work as well as before, but he says he can live with it.

Gordon's will to fight and his faith in God are no doubt a tribute to his parents. Those qualities were instilled in him at the knees of his praying mother and from the teaching of a dad who believed early childhood experiences would have a greater impact on his son than anything stated in words.

The son of Orville and Molly Manning, Gordon was born Aug. 17, 1951, south of Valliant, near Clear Creek. He was named after the doctor who delivered him, Dr. Gordon Welch. His sister, Orvilyn, nineteen years older than he, had already left home by the time Gordon was born.

The son of a minister, Gordon's childhood memories bring back times when it was hard for the family to get by, with never more than just enough for what was needed. He remembers stories about his dad, before he became a minister, when only his mother's prayers helped the family get through the toughest of times. "From what I'm told, my dad was quite a hell-raiser," Gordon grinned, "Mother said he used to play music for dances. I remember her saying that Daddy never could make any money at it because he broke all his guitars and fiddles getting in fights. That was before the Good Lord got a hold of him. After that, Mother said that God changed my daddy, completely."

Gordon was three when the family moved to Haworth, OK where his dad was pastor of the Assembly of God Church. He attended one month in the first grade at Haworth before the family moved back to Valliant and his dad went to work for County Commissioner Marvin McDougal.

Gordon learned about the value of money at a young age. He had two paper routes for both the Daily Oklahoman and Tulsa World. He was about eight when he learned his first lesson in money management. He had seen a Mickey Mouse watch at Merry's Drug Store. "I wanted that watch so bad," Gordon smiled. 'One day, Daddy said, if you want it, go to the bank and borrow the money to buy it. Daddy was a good friend with Ode Cecil, who was the banker at First State Bank. Neal Stuart was the teller. He took me in and we sat down in Ode Cecil's office. We filled out a piece of paper that I thought was a real contract. I needed $5 for the watch and 1 agreed to pay it back at 50 cents a week. That was when 1 started doing business with First State Bank. I guess I must have been a good risk because since that time I have borrowed money from First State to buy boats, airplanes, motorcycles and cars."

"I don't know how old I was when I decided I was going to learn to play a guitar, but Daddy wouldn't buy one for me because he didn't think I could ever learn to play. I cut my finger on a tin can when I was four or five and as a result I couldn't bend my finger. He thought that would prevent me from playing. He wouldn't try to teach me to play either. A lady in our church, Granny Word, we called her, came to our house every Sunday afternoon. She brought her guitar and little amp. She would let me play with it. I would beat on it and she would encourage me. That's how I learned to play a guitar."

"I started saving my money and when I was 12, I bought my first guitar from Sears for $189.95. That was a lot of money back then. I mowed yards and did anything I could to make a dollar. Daddy never did have any money so if I wanted money I had to make my own. From the 7th grade through high school, after I got out of basketball practice in the evenings, I worked as a janitor at Elliott School. When I got big enough for a car, Daddy taught me how to work on one." He said, "Now there you are, son. You keep it running, because I'm not going to."

"All through my high school years, I played in a band for class parties and school dances. Daddy always threatened to kick the speakers out of my amp because he didn't want me to play for dances. I would remind him that he couldn't play for a dance without getting drunk and getting in a fight. I would tell him, 'I never drink, I never do drugs, and I never fight.' And, I'm still playing my first guitar."

"Some of the guys in our band were Gary Milner, Paul Melton, Ronnie Tyler, Boogie Tidmore and Maxey Crouch. I remember one night Maxey's dad came to the American Legion Hut where we were playing for a high school dance. He dragged Maxey off the stage, took him home and locked him in his room. In about 30 minutes Maxey was back, picking and a grinning. He had climbed out of his bedroom window."

The summer after graduating high school, Gordon enrolled at Okmulgee Tech. He finished his degree as an industrial machinist by going straight through one year and two summers.

Weyerhaeuser had just bought out Dierks at Wright City when Gordon landed his first job in the machine shop working for Claude Benson.

When Weyerhaeuser went on strike in 1975, he went to New Orleans, LA and worked for Brown and Root, welding pipe.

After that job ended, he came home and started working for Dwight Francis. A year later, he left for Alaska where he worked for Parker Drilling as a mechanic. He continued to work on drilling rigs off and on for about seven years before coming home and building a boat shop where Buddy Belvins' repair shop is now. He later sold the shop and went back to work for Dwight Francis.

In the meantime, he married Ginger Smith, the daughter of the late Oliver Smith and Bootsie Smith. That was in March 1986. Gordon said way back when there was a height requirement with law enforcement, he wanted to work as a highway patrol officer then, but he was too short. After the limitation was lifted and when he knew they were hiring, he applied. In August 1986, he was hired and assigned to Lake Patrol.

Gordon and Ginger both had children from their first marriages. Ginger's daughter, Emily was two when they married. Gordon's daughter, Alissa was five and his son, Mike was twelve. They raised their children together and Ginger says the three fought each other just the same as blood brothers and sisters do. On the other hand, she said they would fight for each other too.

For 14 years Gordon patrolled the lakes and highways while Ginger pursued her education and began teaching. Their busy lifestyles found them devoting much less time to church and more time to work and other interests, until Gordon's accident brought them to an abrupt realization about, "what is most important."

Even though the accident has taken an emotional and physical toll on both Gordon and Ginger, they agree that more good than bad has come from it. "I had a great job with the highway patrol, one that I enjoyed going to every day," Gordon said, "Now, Ginger and I do more together and we've been happier in the past four years than we ever were before."

Gordon was highly respected as a patrol officer both by his peers as well as his superior officers. He was recognized for many achievements throughout his career.

In August 2001, he received the Oklahoma Highway Patrol Troop Commander's Achievement award. Also, he was presented the Purple Heart due to his accident. Three years ago he and Ginger made a television commercial for Jim Thorpe Rehabilitation Center and in May, 2002, Gordon was asked to be the guest speaker at the Slain Officers Memorial in Austin, TX.

Determined to keep his promise to God, today Gordon visits churches everywhere, sharing his testimony of what God has done for him. Ginger is by his side, using her musical abilities to support his efforts.

My Faithful Friend

By: Viola McEuin

God is not willing that any should perish, but that all should come to repentance.

2 Peter 3:9

This scripture was manifested to me in a very dramatic way in 1979 and 1980. The Lord decided it was time for me to know Him, not just know about Him. I always believed there was a God in Heaven, but I did not know Him. My family rarely went to church. I grew up with little knowledge or teaching of Jesus. I remembered a song from our rare church visits called *How Beautiful Heaven Must Be*. I think we all want to go there. I had never been taught the way of salvation, but He who is the Way had a plan for my family and me.

Beginning on Sept. 2, 1979, He began to work in my life. It was Labor Day weekend and we were camping at Broken Bow Lake with friends. My best friend through high school joined us for the day. The friends we were camped with had a boat. My four-year-old daughter and we three women took the boat for a ride around the lake. It was such an enjoyable ride, seeing the beautiful scenery and enjoying each other's company.

As we approached the shore on our return, the friend who had joined us for only that day was going to get out of the boat and lift the motor up so the rocks wouldn't damage it. She stood up and fell out of the boat really hard. She held onto the front of the boat with a white-knuckle grasp. It scared me!

She looked so pale and her lips were quivering. I asked her if she was all right because I didn't think she was. She walked around as though she was going to lift the motor. She bypassed the motor and went to the other side of the boat, stopped, and her eyes rolled into the back of her head as she fell into the water. I was terrified. I knew I had to get her head up or she would drown. I felt like I was stuck in slow motion, trying to get out of the boat and get to her. She was lifeless. (I was told later that I just shot out of the boat.) I screamed for help as loud as I could for the men in the camp to come help. They got here quickly and tried CPR until the ambulance arrived. The EMS personnel continued CPR for a long time. It seemed like an hour to me but to no avail. They finally told us there was no heartbeat. My friend, my dearest friend, on earth was gone. I tried to pray for her while they were trying to save her. I sensed the Lord's presence and heard him say, "Don't worry about her, she is in My hands, but you are not My child. You need to know me more."

My heart was shattered and my legs felt like rubber. I couldn't stand and could hardly breath. We had to live through the agony of telling her family that she had died while with us. She had four sisters, a brother, and parents who loved her dearly. The funeral was a blur to me. I lived in a fog and my family was worried about me so my husband took me to the doctor. He gave me some pills for my nerves and they made me want to sleep all the time. When I woke up, the first thing I would see was my dead friend's face. I had a home, a job, a child, and a husband to care for. One day as I headed to work, I fell asleep at the wheel. I veered from the right lane across to the left lane headed toward the ditch. The ditches there are rather deep and sometimes hold water. The Lord protected us and the car stayed right at the edge of the road. I woke up to the sight of tall grass coming up onto the hood of the car. I hit the brakes and miracle of miracles; neither my husband nor I had a scratch. There was grass all over the car and under the hood but it wasn't scratched either. Cars were lined up on the road, stopping to see if we were hurt. I could have killed several people that morning. At that moment, I realized the enemy of my soul was out to destroy me.

I began praying, asking God to help me. "Please God, help me to know you and please help me to take care of my family." From that time on I was determined to start going to church. My husband fought that decision for a while. I felt that the Lord said, "You go to church and take your daughter and learn of Me. I will take care of your husband." It wasn't long before he was going with us. We learned of the Lord together as a family. We learned that Jesus died for our sins and that no man comes to the Father except through faith in Jesus Christ, His Son.

On February 29, 1980, we watched a film called, *Judgment Day,* at the Assembly of God church in Valliant, Okla. After viewing that film, I promised God, that with His help, I would serve Him all the days of my life. He has helped me and for 35 years I have kept that promise. My daughter and granddaughter know the Lord because God cared enough to spare my life until I knew Him. Jesus has been my best friend; He is everything I will ever need. My husband waits for me in Heaven. I hope my friend is there. We had never talked about God so I can only hope she is there.

I give praise to my faithful friend, Jesus, who spared my life until I came to know Him. I pray daily to be a faithful follower of Him, until that day that I see Him face to face.

Roaring Lion of Judah

By: Viola McEuin

On October 31, 2011 I had a third recurrent ventral hernia surgery at Paris Regional Hospital in Paris, TX. Although these surgeries are hard to go through and take awhile to recover from, I was doing well until the seventh day after surgery. I had gotten a sinus infection as I usually do because of the drainage tube that goes through my nose to my stomach. I was really sick. When my daughter called before she went to Sunday school that morning, I told her to take care of herself and her daughter and that I loved them. I really felt like I was on my way out of this world.

That really upset my family. They went to church early for the prayer meeting at 9:15 a.m. My daughter asked for prayer for me and reported that I had basically said goodbye, even though Christians never really have to say goodbye. Everyone at Broken Bow First Assembly prayed for all requests at that time.

I don't know what time the doctor came in to see me. I told him I was so sick that I could hardly hold my head up. It seemed to surprise him since I had been up and around and doing fairly well in the previous days. He said he would take the tube out and maybe that would help. I said, "Oh, praise God!"

After the doctor left and before the nurse came in to remove the tube, I heard a tremendously loud roar in my room. It sounded so ferocious and yet I wasn't frightened by it at all. I recognized my Savior and said, "Oh, it's the Lion of Judah". I had also recognized the enemy who goes around as a roaring lion, seeking whom he may devour. I sensed him slither away. It occurred to me that he was helpless against the "Roaring Lion of Judah", my Redeemer, Protector, and Deliverer. I will never forget it as long as I live.

Almost immediately, I felt so much better. I was so glad to get that tube out of my nose. After expelling some of the infection, I was able to stand with shaky legs, shampoo my hair and bathe. Then, I collapsed into bed for a beautiful time of restful sleep. What peace we can have knowing our life is in God's hands and He is for us, always.

When my daughter called after church, I told her how much better I was and we rejoiced and thanked God together. God answered the prayers of my church family in a prayer circle. The Lion of Judah fought for me, protected me, and healed me quickly. I steadily got better. I was released to go home three days later.

I will never forget how powerful He was, is, and always will be. One of my church sisters gave me a little statue of the Lion of Judah she had. She said I needed it because of my testimony. I have it on a shelf where I can see it often and thank Him again for caring for a widow lady like me. I am His and He is mine. Thank You, powerful Lion of Judah. I will praise You forever.

Christy and God's Visible Grace

By: Frank Meddock

It was a dark Halloween night; it seemed that it was as dark as it could get. I, with a standard two-cell flashlight, had been walking and following alongside a trailer lined with bales of hay and loaded with kids on a Halloween hayride. I had taken my daughter Lorrie Kaye to her friend's house to participate in the Halloween party. Bill Bailey, the dad and host, asked me to stay long enough to help with the hayride. Bill had the trailer loaded with hay and hooked to a big green tractor, not John Deere, but Deutz. The German made tractor could have pulled ten of the trailers being used that night. The kids were running in all directions having a good time.

The shadows of the evening were coming over the trees in the backyard of the Bailey's home when Bill gave the command for the kids to load up. I don't know the number of kids on the trailer, but it was loaded. I was given the flashlight and the kids were cautioned to stay seated. By the time everyone was placed on the trailer and ready to go, it was quite dark. Bill started the tractor and we headed out on the preplanned route that lead through a dense, dark, wooded area not far from the Bailey's home.

The night was dark, really dark. I was walking to the left side and to the rear of the trailer. The beam of the flashlight cut a small hole into the dark night. The kids were frolicking and making lots of noise as if they had seen or were expecting to see a ghost or maybe a big black cat.

The winding trails led us through the woods and back out into the open area and then turned back toward the house. A fence and cattle guard separated the wooded and pasture area from the outside property of the residence. As we approached the cattle guard crossing at the fence, the tractor came to an abrupt stop as though it had run into something. The driver got down off the tractor and went to the front to see what had stopped the tractor. I walked part way to the front. One of the other dads met me part way and said the front wheel had fallen into a hole. I turned back toward the trailer, as the small round beam of the light fell on the trailer and kids. It was at the bottom edge of the light beam.

In the darkness of the night, I caught a glimpse of something under the trailer. The first thing I saw was the brown fur coat of a child extruding from behind the tires and under the trailer. The child was face down under the trailer. Her blonde hair mingled with the brown fur on the coat. Her head and shoulders were protruding somewhat from under the left front tire of the tandem wheeled trailer. I went to the ground before the child. The tire was flattened out over and around her. She was face down, but as I hunkered to the ground before her, she was looking at me, into the light. The look on her face and in her eyes was invincible. I will never be able to explain except that I had seen that look once before. I don't remember the mechanics of removing her from under the wheel except that it was intricate. It was almost like a dream. I was not sure it was really happening. The tire was flattened out over and around the child (no air) but it didn't seem to have a gripping hold on her. I removed her from under the tire without having to forcefully pull on her in any way that would have further injured her. After standing her before me, and with the dim light, I recognized that it was Christy Carver, my daughter Lorrie Kaye's friend.

I stood Christy in front of me and was trying to communicate with her to know the seriousness of her injuries. Christy was not answering me. She wasn't saying anything. She just stood there with the very strange look in her eyes. I hardly noticed as the tractor and trailer were pulling away.

The driver and the other dads were not aware of what had happened. They had observed that the tractor had hit something, and they were assuming it must have been the hole near the cattle guard, or perhaps the actual cattle guard. After reviewing the cattle guard and the hole at the front of the tractor, they saw nothing to keep the tractor from going on. They simply drove on toward the house.

Christy eventually began to talk, which comforted me to some extent that she was okay. We walked toward the house together. By the time we got to the house, the other kids had dispersed from the trailer and appeared to be having a good time. As Christy and I arrived at the house, we told the others what had happened, with me mostly doing the talking and Christy standing by my side. It seemed that they didn't hear what we were saying. They would say something like, "Oh that is good", "I'm glad she didn't get hurt." They then changed the subject and walked away. I told Bill what happened after that, and he seemed alarmed to know that she could have been seriously injured, but no one seemed to comprehend what had really happened.

The tractor could have hit the hole and the cattle guard, and never slowed down or come to a sudden stop. If the tractor had gone another six inches, Christy would have been under the steel of the tire, instead of just the flattened rubber tire. I know the tire was not flat when we left the house. While back at the house and in the lights, I further observed Christy and her demeanor while still wondering if she was okay. She didn't appear to be cut, bruised, or even unusually dirty. Christy disappeared into the group of girls, and I went on my way.

It has been more than twenty years since, and Christy has grown up and has a family of her own. She is doing well. I had assumed that she had fallen from the front of the trailer all those years ago, but after recalling that night with Christy, she claims someone pushed her! The memory of Christy looking at me from under the flattened tire of the trailer comes to my mind more often than it should. Because of that, I have wondered if I should tell others of what I have seen, believing it was "GOD'S VISIBLE GRACE."

I might further explain, as I earlier mentioned that I had seen that invincible look once before. The same look on a child's face, as though it was the same person. Concerning that event, it was about five years earlier. I was standing on the sidewalk near the back of my furniture store in Broken Bow, Oklahoma. I heard the squeal of tires that had locked up on the nearby highway. Knowing something must be wrong, I ran the distance of a city block to the highway and around the corner. There were skid marks leading to the car, sitting in the middle of the highway. The lady in the car was screaming frantically. She was visibly terrified at what had happened. I looked under the car from the front bumper area. A young child was under the car between the front wheels and under the motor section of the car. The child turned and looked at me with that exact look. I pulled the child, who I later found out to be Clayton Bruner, out from under the car. He was about eight years old.

Clayton's father was our tax accountant and Clayton was also a friend of Stephen, my son. I asked others to call his parents and then decided to take him to the hospital myself. I don't remember who it was that went with us, who was driving, or even what we were driving. I just remember the look on Clayton's face while he was under that car. It was the look I also saw on Christy's face. In both situations, the children wouldn't speak to me. We were approaching the hospital when Clayton started to speak again. They kept him in the hospital for a few hours and checked him over well. They found no serious injuries.

I have since looked under the front bumper of vehicles similar to the car that was involved. There is no room for a child to fit without sustaining some injuries. I can't with common sense explain it. I have decided that the Lord may visibly show us His grace and His power. If we witness these acts, we should not keep them to ourselves, but share what we have seen with others, so that they would also be encouraged, being reminded of GOD'S REAL AND PRESENT GRACE.

Angels of the Lord

By: Daisy Nix

The angel of the lord encampeth round about them fear Him and delivereth them.

Psalms 34:7

My husband, Dub, and I were on our way to Oklahoma City. In Shawnee, on a four-lane highway, I was approaching a traffic signal. I was driving fifty-five mph, and the light had just turned green. I didn't slow down. A young man, driving a diesel truck and pulling a trailer, turned left in front of me. The collision was inevitable.

The windshield on the passenger side broke and the shattered glass got in Dub's face. The airbags were released and they bruised my hands. Other than that, we had no injuries, but our car was totaled. The other driver was not injured either. God's angels are always around us, protecting us when we are not aware of it. Glendell, our son, came and picked us up and took us on to the city. The Lord helped us get another car while we were there. I got in the new car and drove the two hundred plus miles back home. The Lord helped me overcome the fear Satan tried to put on me. I've been driving ever since.

The Lord, Our Deliverer

By: Daisy Nix

"Many are the afflictions of the righteous, but the Lord delivereth them out of all their troubles."

Psalms 34:19

My husband, Dub, was diagnosed with colon cancer and was receiving treatments in Texarkana, TX. One day he was sent for a CT scan and he was allowed to return home that same day. That evening he got very sick and I took him to the ER and they put him in the hospital. They called the clinic where the CT scan was done. The results showed his colon was twisted. They told me that he was so weak from the chemotherapy that nothing could be done about it. A deacon from our church, Brother Greg Gulich, came by and we prayed. God performed a miracle. The colon untwisted and Dub was healed. He did fine through the rest of his treatments and the cancer has never returned. We give God all the glory.

Many times in my life God has brought inner peace to my heart in troubled times. Intercessory prayer has been used to intervene on behalf of my family. God's love and protection has always been there for us.

My Journey, My Testimony

By: Glenda Gilbert Sandridge

In November 1999, my world as I knew it changed forever. My husband of 33 ½ years went in for his routine yearly physical exam. After a routine chest x-ray, the doctor ordered additional testing the same day and my husband was diagnosed with renal cell carcinoma (kidney cancer). Our daughter Jamie called and gave me a scripture. Isaiah 41:10 says, *"Fear thou not; For I am with thee; Be not dismayed; For I am thy God; I will strengthen thee: Yea, I will help thee; Yea, I will uphold thee with the right hand of my righteousness"*. He lived six and a half months and passed away on May 24, 2000. Five months after he passed away, my doctor scheduled some routine tests for me. In October 2000, I was diagnosed with colon cancer. The Lord was faithful and saw me through the surgery and I was given a clean bill of health. I did not have to have any further treatment except for the colonoscopies that were necessary to make sure I stayed cancer free. I knew God was with me.

In 2009 I became my brother's caregiver. For the next few years, I devoted my time to Phillip. He had severe heart problems and had to live with a heart pump (LVAD) implanted inside him. In April 2013, I knew I had something different going on in my left breast. I didn't want to tell him about my situation, but I decided to go to my doctor for a mammogram and a sonogram. The doctor that came in to check on the findings of the sonogram said he didn't see anything to be concerned about. That was good news for me so I was not concerned. On July 10, 2013, we had to get hospice care for my brother. He was staying with me and the nurses were with him around the clock. Our mother, Louise Gilbert, called him from Oklahoma to check on his condition and she told me she had released him to the Lord that day. That afternoon he began to get worse. When I went to the door that night to let the night shift nurse in, he said, "Hello, my name is Gabriel." This nurse had never been here before. The Lord let me know He was in control. My brother passed away on July 26, 2013.

It has now been 14 and a half years since my husband passed away and three months since my brother passed. I knew that whatever was wrong in my left breast in April was getting larger. On October 18, I went to my gynecologist. She sent me for another mammogram and sonogram the same day. I called my best friend Charlotte Snider to ask her to go with me. She agreed and said she would be there right away. She is the kind of friend everyone needs. She is a prayer warrior and trusts in the Lord for everything. The doctor read the sonogram after my second test and said we needed a biopsy done. On Friday, October 25, I received the call no one wants to get. The doctor said, "Glenda you have breast cancer." I was diagnosed with an invasive lobular carcinoma. I was shocked and cried at the news. I called three of my dear friends (Charlotte Snider, Linda Singleton and Linda Simmons) and they came over to pray with me. At that moment, the Lord gave me a peace that only He can give. All the fear I had left. I can truly say that the peace I received from the Lord is still with me today. During my Sunday school class, later that week, we were taking prayer requests and my cousin's husband said, "Glenda needs prayer."

Ladies gathered around me and began to pray. A gentleman at the front of the class stood up and looked straight at me. He said, "The Lord has shown me He is going to take care of you. I saw the Lord's hand go over your body." He demonstrated what he saw on his own body. Brother Green started on his left side and went all over his body down to his legs. My problem was on my left side. After Sunday school, another gentlemen named Brother Jones came up to me and said the Holy Spirit told him I was going to be taken care of. Brother Jones has now gone to be with the Lord. The sermon in church that morning was "God Goes Before Us". My daughter called and said the sermon in her church that morning was "God is Able". We both knew the Lord was in control. That night at church, Brother Green came up to me and said when he tried to take his afternoon nap; all he could see was the Lord's hand going over me again.

I have a few scriptures that I depend on in my Bible. I have written beside Psalms 120:1, (THE PROBLEM) *"In my distress, I cried unto the Lord and He heard me."* In Psalms 121: 1-8, I have written (THE ANSWER), *"I will lift up mine eyes unto the hills from which cometh my help. My help cometh from the Lord, which made heaven and earth. He will not suffer thy foot to be moved, he that keepeth thee will not slumber. Behold, he that keepeth Israel shall neither slumber nor sleep. The Lord is thy keeper the Lord is thy shade upon thy right hand. The sun shall not smite thee by day, nor the moon by night. The Lord shall preserve thee from all evil; he shall preserve thy soul. The Lord shall preserve thy going out and thy coming in from this time forth, and even for evermore.* WHAT A PROMISE!

The following Monday, I went to see the surgeon. The news was not good. I would have to have my left breast removed. The next day I had additional tests ran on me. I had MRIs, CAT scans, bone scans, and more biopsies. In my "Jesus Calling" devotion book that next morning, I noticed the words on the paper. They said, "I am with you, I am with you, I am with you". This was another promise of the Lord's presence. The surgeon called with the results of the scans. They showed that the cancer had not spread to any other organs or to my bones. The MRI showed it to be a little smaller then what she measured in her office. However, a couple of places were identified in my right breast. I had to have more biopsies.

One of the hardest things I had to do was go to Oklahoma and tell my 88 year-old mother. She had just lost my brother three months prior. On October 31, Linda Singleton, my mother's sister-in-law and a jewel of a person, and I went to break the news. My church was praying for this situation and I was reminded of the pastor's sermon, "God Goes Before Us" and He did. Mother handled it great. On November 5, I had more biopsies. When it was over, the nurse asked me who I had with me. I said, "Two Linda's and a Charlotte." I am told that is how they called them back to the recovery room.

Three days later, the doctor called with my results. I would have to have both breasts removed. The cancer had also spread to my lymph nodes. For the next few weeks, I was going from doctor to doctor. On December 3, 2013, I had to have a nuclear injection to get ready for the lymph node surgery scheduled for the next day. It was the most painful thing that I went through. Five days after my lymph nodes were removed, I had a double mastectomy. I was cut halfway around my body. I also had to have more lymph nodes removed on the left side during that surgery. I had some issues with the anesthesia after the surgery. I could not move my arms or legs. During the surgery, or sometime when I was coming out from under the anesthesia, I remember seeing my brother who had passed away. Very softly, I heard him call my name and when I turned and looked he was standing on a very beautiful green pathway looking back at me. Later, he loudly called my name again, but I could not see him. During this time, two songs kept coming to me. One of them was " I Go To The Rock." Some of the verses in this song say, "Who can I go to? Who can I turn to? When I need a shelter, when I need a friend, I go to the Rock. When everything around me is sinking sand, Christ the solid Rock I stand." I am so grateful he has been and is my Rock. The other song that kept coming to me was "Nothing But The Blood". No words came to me just the words, "Nothing But The Blood." I know the blood will never lose its power. There is power in the blood. What can wash away my sins? The Blood. It is my protection. Scripture says, "When I see the blood, I will pass over you." What can make me whole again? Jesus paid the price with His blood and it still works. The Lord has promised us He will never leave us nor forsake us.

One month to the day from my surgery, on January 9, 2014 my mother-in-law, Audrey Sandridge, went home to be with the Lord. I never told her what I was going through. I called the nursing home daily checking on her. Donita Clay was an angel and had visited her in the nursing home when I could not. She helped me take care of the funeral arrangements via telephone.

I started chemotherapy in January of 2014 and finished that June. I lost all of my hair and believe it or not, it is not so bad. I also had twenty-eight radiation treatments (5 days a week for 5 ½ weeks). The Lord was with me every step of the way. He had promised to go before me and He always did. The chemo never made me sick, only weak at times. I would pray and ask the Lord to cover the chemo with His blood before it went through me. The Lord gave me a scripture during this time: *Isaiah 53:5, "But He was wounded for our transgressions, He was bruised for our iniquities, the chastisement of our peace was upon him and WITH HIS*

STRIPES WE ARE HEALED." That is a promise. I met a lot of people at chemo that were a lot worse off than me. Some have been given a death sentence.

We do not know why we go through some of the things we go through, but the Lord knows, and He cares about each and every one of them. During this bump in my road, not only did I lose my mother-in-law, but in February, my niece Lisa Coleman Fuentes (my sister and brother-in-law's only child) passed away unexpectedly. She had just turned 52. In August, my cousin Glen Curry passed away.

I have tried to witness about what the Lord has done and is doing for me to everyone I meet. My wig and ball caps have been a good topic for witnessing. If I never get all of my hair back, that is okay also. It has been one year since my journey began, and I am doing great. I feel good. My chemotherapy doctor does not want to see me again for six months. I have one more surgery to go through, but it has not been scheduled as of yet.

My mom called me the other day and witnessed to me over the phone. She is now 89 and witnesses through song. She sang, "HE WILL NEVER LET GO OF MY HAND. THOUGH THE STORMS MAY COME AND THE WINDS MAY BLOW, HE WILL ALWAYS WALK CLOSE TO ME."

There is a song that says, "After a while it will all be over", and it will be. Then we will all sing, "WHAT A DAY THAT WILL BE WHEN MY JESUS I SHALL SEE. WHEN I LOOK UPON HIS FACE THE ONE WHO SAVED ME BY HIS GRACE."

I thank the Lord everyday for what He has done for me and what He continues to do. I have heard people that have gone through a terrible situation say that if they had to do it all over again, they would. I never understood that; but now I do. I always knew I loved the Lord, but I can truly say I love Him and I am closer to Him than I have ever been. I want to be His hand extended so others will know and believe. My scripture is: 2 Timothy 1:12, "For the which cause I also suffer these things, nevertheless I am not ashamed: FOR I KNOW WHOM I HAVE BELIEVED AND AM PERSUADED THAT HE IS ABLE TO KEEP THAT WHICH I HAVE COMMITTED UNTO HIM AGAINST THAT DAY."

The Lord truly is my Rock and my Salvation.

Apple for Christmas

By: Brent Schreckhise

*I*n the early 1980s, a shipping embargo resulted in some supply shortages in the country of Honduras. We had lived in Honduras as missionaries for around ten years and had learned to adapt to the differences we faced being away from the United States. However, my parents tried to make certain occasions special for us boys. One of those occasions was Christmas.

My mom loved to make our Christmas special. At that time, we didn't travel back and forth as freely to the United States as we do now. She would often buy Christmas gifts two or three years in advance and store them until that special day.

One of our favorite traditions was her special candied apples. Every year, she searched for those large Red Delicious apples that were imported from the U.S, and she would make enough for all of us to enjoy. The apples were such a treat.

This particular year, no apples could be found because of the embargo. My parents searched all over the capital city of Tegucigalpa for them, but no apples could be found. We couldn't believe it. No apples? Would it be Christmas really without those candied apples?

A couple of days before Christmas, we traveled to Tela, a seaside village where we would spend the holidays. One night we talked about the fact that we wouldn't have any candied apples. My mom said, "Boys, let's pray. God can provide us with apples." So before we went to bed, we prayed. Then we went to sleep.

The next morning, we got up early to go swimming at the beach. My older brother Brad and I waded out into the water. We were having a great time splashing around when I felt something bump me in the back.

My first thought was shark, but imagine my surprise when I whipped around to see a large Red Delicious apple floating in the water. I grabbed it and turned it toward my brother to show him. At the same moment, he held up an apple to show me. When we looked around, there were Red Delicious apples floating on the waves all the way around us. We gathered about two dozen apples from the water that day. When we took them back to the cabin to show our mom, she was excited to see how the Lord answered our prayers. After she prepared the candied apples, we savored every bite. As children, we learned that God cares about even the little things in our lives.

A Home of My Own

By: Jennifer Schreckhise

Every woman loves the thought of having a home of her own and I was no exception. After several years on the mission field, I longed to have a place to call my own.

Since leaving Broken Bow, Oklahoma not long after our marriage, we had moved 11 times. Our latest move had us living in a very small house in the city of La Ceiba, Honduras, with our family of nine. Enclosed in the high walls that surrounded our house was a tiny yard for our children to play. It was to this yard I retreated when it felt like the walls were closing in on me. I can remember looking up into the sky asking the Lord for a home with a large yard where our children could play. I told Him I would love for it to be in the country, and that my dream property would even have a little creek.

In the country of Honduras (at that time) it was impossible for a foreigner to obtain a mortgage for a home. With an asking price of $125,000 for a 1200 square foot house, the inability to get a loan made my desire for a home seem impossible. I came to the point that I told the Lord, "Ok, Lord I will serve you joyfully whether I ever have my own home or not." The desire was still there but I was willing to accept God's will for our family.

About a month later as we were driving through the country, we noticed a large lot for sale. We called to ask about it. The price was within our reach and best of all, at the back of the property was a little creek. The lot boasted several cocoa and mango trees. It was beautiful.

After praying, we made the purchase. We started to sketch house plans and figuring how many cement blocks it would take to build a house. A few weeks later on a trip to the U.S. my husband, Brent, was sharing our excitement with a pastor friend of ours in Scottsdale, Arizona. The pastor told his congregation that he wanted the church to be able to give the first $1000 toward our new home. What an unexpected blessing! We were on our way.

From there Brent went to California. As he was driving to a conference with some friends, they saw a garage sale sign. When they pulled up, Brent spotted some appliances that were exactly what I had described that I wanted for our new kitchen someday. The gentlemen selling them said they were barely used. Although his wife rarely cooked, she wanted new stainless steel appliances.

He said he would take $200 for everything; the cooktop, wall oven, microwave, and dishwasher. Brent called me and said, "I know we don't have our house yet, but I found all the appliances you wanted for just $200. After Brent returned, he hired some men to start digging the foundation for our home. He told me, "We are going to trust God to build this house. We are not going to go into debt. We are not going to ask our supporters for any extra money. Let's see what God will do."

God has amazed us many times in the years since we began our home. One church helped us put up walls. Another congregation donated windows. One church sent an electrician and a cabinetmaker to help with the finishing details. Just when it seemed we would have to stop because of lack of funds, someone would call with a desire to help us with our new house. We have been blessed by so many dear friends and churches throughout the United States and Canada.

We have lived in our newly built home for three years. It is beautiful and spacious. There is a tire swing in the mango tree and the yard is big enough for a rousing game of *futbol* with the neighborhood kids. There is enough room for the chickens, the dogs, a cat, and the rabbits. We often tell our children, "This house does not belong to us. This is God's house." And just like God's amazing provision has never failed us, the little creek in the back never stops running, even in the driest months.

A Watermelon in the Mailbox

By: Jennifer Schreckhise

When I was expecting my second child, we lived in the city of Yuma, Arizona. It is always hot and dry in Yuma, and I was a bit miserable in my condition. One day after service, I overheard someone mention that they were going home to eat cold watermelon. Oh, just the thought of that cold watermelon made my mouth water. I couldn't get the craving for watermelon out of my mind.

After everyone left, I asked my husband if we could get a watermelon. I remember him saying, "We don't have any money for one, but we can pray." I don't remember praying a fervent prayer for watermelon that day, but God knows the desires of our heart. The next day I was in the kitchen when Brent walked in with a HUGE watermelon. I asked, "Where in the world did that come from?" He said, "It was in the mailbox." What? How?

That Tuesday, Brent was at the mailbox when the mail carrier came. When he asked her about the watermelon, she admitted to putting it in our mailbox. "But why?" asked Brent. She said, "It was the strangest thing. When I was delivering mail around the corner at the fruit stand, I saw the watermelon and felt I should buy it. Ok, I thought, my kids and my husband like watermelon, I'll take it home to them. But when I got to your house, the Holy Spirit told me to put it in your mailbox, so I did."

That was one of the best watermelons we've ever eaten. I'm not sure it met all the postal codes, but it was amazing answer to a heart's desire.

Awakened by the Lord

By: Bob Studer

I was working at the Weyerhauser mill in Wright City, OK and was working high in the air when I fell seventeen feet down to a concrete floor. I was rushed to the DeQueen, Arkansas hospital and put into intensive care for seven to nine days.

Every rib was smashed in the front portion of my chest and I was put on a respirator that kept me breathing. The doctor went through my back to remove the blood from my lungs.

My pelvis was broken in five places. The ball in my right hip joint was broken in half. Both bones in my forearm were also broken, along with my wrist.

My two eldest brothers, who lived in Michigan came to see me. The doctors were only allowing one person in to see me every six hours. The oldest brother was complaining that they had driven over a thousand miles to see me, and they weren't being let in. "Well, go on in. He probably won't live until morning," said the doctor when he finally allowed them in.

The nurse heard the doctor's words and she decided to call some people at the Assembly of God church in DeQueen. She called for a 36-hour prayer vigil for me. The doctors said I would never walk again and that I'd have to have an operation on my pelvis within six months. It has been about 40 years since then, and I haven't had an operation yet.

My body absorbed half of the ball that was broken off in my hip and fluid was put in, which the doctors had never seen happen before. I was out for around six days when a storm came and the respirator that kept me breathing shut off from a power outage. My eyes flew open and one of the nurses said that the Lord had woken me up. I praised the Lord for watching over me and healing me.

*Bob Studer returned to work six months after the accident and continued to work till his retirement in 2000.

Call on the Name of Jesus

By: Lavon Studer

It was Christmas time. My husband, Bob, and I went to Edinburg, TX; just ten miles form the Mexican border, to visit our son Joe and his wife Ludy. We eagerly anticipated the trip as we only get to see them about once a year.

After a very pleasant day of sightseeing we stopped at a fish café for dinner. Joe, Ludy, and Bob had all gotten out of the car and were waiting on me. I was slow getting out. When I went around the back of the car I stumbled or stepped on something that caused me to lose my balance. I started running and could not stop. I fell face down on the curb. My nose was bleeding so bad that they called an ambulance. As I lay there waiting for the ambulance, I kept calling on the name of Jesus. I knew in my spirit that He had heard me and spared me from a more serious injury.

We had to wait for the doctor a long time after we reached the hospital but after he finally got there he did a wonderful job of repairing my nose. It had almost been torn off by the impact with the curb. My left leg was also injured but not broken, and my shoulders were also hurt. I had to exercise a lot to regain my mobility.

We had to stay in Edinburg for almost four months while my nose healed and the stitches could be removed. Today you can barely see the scar from my injury. After doing a lot of exercise, walking and riding my stationery bicycle, I can get around in my house. For safety sake, I use a cane, a walker, or Bob's arm when I go out. I never want to fall on concrete again.

Today I am so thankful to the Lord for sparing me from a more serious injury.

Thank You, Lord

By: Carol Swift

For many years, we had raised chickens and had two large chicken houses. It was winter time and extremely cold. I went to the chicken house to tack a large piece of plastic over the big doors located at the end of the building to help keep the building warm for the chickens. I was up on a 10-foot ladder trying to check to make sure the plastic was in place. I was on the next to the top step of the ladder. I knew that it was not a wise or safe step to be on, but I knew I had to protect our investment.

The ladder started to fall. I cried out, "Help, God." I heard a voice say, "Don't stick your hands or feet out." I just hung on and rode the ladder down. I landed so softly and gently that the impact did not even knock my glasses off. I wasn't hurt at all. I was so grateful I just kept saying, "Thank you Lord, thank you so much."

Psalms 34: 7-17, "The righteous cry, and the Lord hearth, and deliverer with them out of all their troubles."

Made in the USA
Monee, IL
07 June 2022